Your Visit to the Shrine

of Sainte-Anne de Beaupré

Samuel Baillargeon, C.Ss.R.

With the Approval of Church Authority

All Rights Reserved

Translated from the French by: Gabriel Bergeron

ISBN - 2 - 89238 - 303- X

Printed in Canada

NINTH PART OF THE VISIT:
THE CHOIR LOFT OF THE BASILICA   137

TENTH PART OF THE VISIT:
THE CHAPEL OF THE IMMACULATE CONCEPTION   138

Before you start visiting the Basilica, we beg you to read the following message:

1. WHAT SAINTE-ANNE-DE-BEAUPRÉ MEANS TO US...

The Basilica with its surroundings is not just one tourist attraction among others; it is a place of worship, of faith and Church gathering.

A **SYMBOL OF FAITH**... To all the Christians of America, the Basilica of Sainte-Anne-de-Beaupré is a visible sign of faith. When one undertakes "his visit to Saint Ann", he is conscious of doing something different from the ordinary practice of a believer.

A **HIGH PLACE OF WORSHIP**... High quality distinguishes the devout visitor's behavior. Constant use of the Sacraments, Holy Mass attendance, private devotions, candlelight processions and the like are all signs of the high quality worship displayed here by the fervent pilgrims. To visitors, this place symbolizes Our Lord's presence and Saint Ann's kindness.

A **GATHERING WITH THE LORD**... Acts of faith and prayer are usually performed in important gatherings called group pilgrimages. This kind of collective worship favors a more abundant effusion of faith. Large crowds of believers praying Our Lord and Good Saint Ann provide some sort of Church atmosphere, a certain religious experience in which faith is tempered anew.

2. WHEN VISITING THE SHRINE AND ITS SURROUNDINGS, YOU ARE KINDLY REQUESTED TO RESPECT THE ATMOSPHERE ᐧOF FAITH AND PRAYER WHICH PERVADES THIS PLACE, IN THE FOLLOWING WAY:

a. When there is a *religious office* going on in the Basilica or elsewhere, please do not stroll nearby.
b. Keep respectfully silent where advisable.
c. Do not take photographs during offices.
d. Come dressed as befits the place where you are.

1. THE BASILICA SQUARE

(To begin your visit, we recommend that you go to the square in front of the Basilica. Since the visit of the Basilica will take a good deal of time, you had better look at the monuments in the square before going inside.)

1. THE FIRST CHURCH SITE

A commemorative plaque has been set up by the Commission for Historical Monuments, a few feet away from the wall separating the square from the street. The inscription says:

> "The first church of Sainte-Anne-de-Beaupré was erected here in 1658".

It was on March 13, 1658, that Reverend Guillaume Vignal, a priest acting on behalf of Sir Thubières de Queylus, Sulpician and parish priest of Quebec, "blessed the site of the Petit-Cap chuch", as it is related in the Jesuit Journal. Governor M. d'Ailleboust "laid the first stone".

2. THE MONUMENTAL STATUE OF SAINT ANN

In the middle of the square, stands a *monumental statue* of Saint Ann, Mary's mother. A Canadian sculptor, Émile Brunet, carved this statue which was installed in the center of a fountain in 1959. The gushing water overflows from two superimposed basins, the larger of which is 32 feet in diameter.

The bronze statue is 9 feet high and represents Saint Ann teaching the Virgin; Mary holds a scroll on which is written the Latin word "Caritas" for Charity.

> "I have also begun a study of the expression of Saint Ann's face, looking for meekness and kindness. Saint Ann would be about 45 years of age and the Virgin, three". (Émile Brunet, March 10, 1958, ASA, B-11d, b.2/doc. 3668-7)

"Since Saint Ann's statue will be set up in Canada, I thought the Canadian spirit would require a crown of maple leaves to be

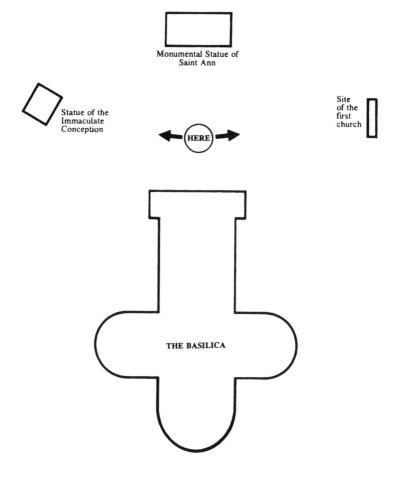

Monumental Statue of
Saint Ann

Statue of the
Immaculate
Conception

HERE

Site
of the
first
church

THE BASILICA

made as a tribute to Saint Ann and the Holy Virgin". (Émile Brunet, June 3, 1958, ASA, B-11d, b.2/doc. 3668-9)

3. THE STATUE OF THE IMMACULATE CONCEPTION

A place of honor has also been provided for our Mother, the Virgin Mary. The nine-foot statue is of cast iron covered with bronze paint and was made by the Vaucouleurs Cast Iron Co. of France, a firm known here by the name of "Union Internationale des Artistes". When it was first placed in the square, the monumental statue was about where Saint Ann's fountain stands now. Bishop J. Alfred Langlois solemnly blessed this statue of the Immaculate Conception on May 1, 1932. Since June 1958, it rests in a shaded corner of the square where sick pilgrims gather during the July novena to say the Rosary.

2. THE FACADE OF THE BASILICA

A. A BRIEF HISTORY OF THE CONSTRUCTION OF THE BASILICA

Before beginning the detailed visit of the Basilica, you ought to know some general data about this building.

1. The Architects:

This church was built to replace the "old Basilica" destroyed by fire on March 29, 1922. A committee of architects was promptly organized to prepare the construction of the new Basilica. The two chief architects were *Maxime Roisin* of Paris, France and *Louis-N. Audet* of Sherbrooke, Québec.

2. The Dimensions:

The building covers an area of 45,000 square feet. The maximum measurements of the Basilica are as follows:

325 feet in length, measured from the exterior
200 feet in width at the transept
300 feet in height at the cross on top of the steeples
160 feet in width at the facade.

The numbers 325, 300 and 200 are easy to remember when giving the main dimensions of the building.

3. The Style of the Basilica:

Following an old tradition in church design, the general floor plan of the Basilica is in the shape of a Latin cross, with the transepts as the arms. According to Louis-N. Audet's own expression, "it is a church of neo-Romanesque style". It means that this church was built with modern techniques of construction, but was decorated in the traditional manner of Romanesque cathedrals. The church is supported by a steel framework and firm foundations laid on solid rock 15 feet below the ground. These were necessary to support the enormous mass of the structure made of white granite from Saint Sébastien in Beauce. The architectural decoration is based on typical Romanesque lines, with the round arch appearing everywhere outside as well as inside. Let us bear in mind, however, that in the present type of structure, a technically perfect arrangement of stone blocks in counter-balanced arches, vaults, walls and buttresses is not necessary to support the building, as was the case with the ancient Romanesque cathedrals. Here, the building holds together thanks to a firm steel framework wrapped in stone.

4. Chronology of the Construction of the Basilica:

You will find here a year-to-year account of the different stages of the construction work. You may want to refer to it as to a kind of memorandum during your visit. But, anyone who reads this detailed record with attention, will realize how much patience and relentless effort were required to assure constant progress in such a complex undertaking.

1922	March 29	The first Basilica is destroyed by fire.
1922	May 27	The temporary church is opened for worship.
1922	Sept. to Dec.	The old Basilica is being demolished.
1922	September 27	The statue is taken down from the gable.
1922	October	F.X. Lambert is chosen as contractor and foreman for the construction of the new Basilica.

The Basilica of Sainte-Anne-de-Beaupré

This photograph taken from the hill gives a clear idea of the Latin-cross design adopted for the construction of the church. In the foreground, the Redemptorist Fathers Monastery.

1923	March 17	A first draft of the new Basilica is brought out by the architects committee.
1923	July 6	Excavation work begins.
1923	July 26	Blessing of the cornerstone.
1923	October 18	L.A. Bussières of Saint-Sébastien, Beauce, obtains the granite laying contract for the future construction.
1924	February	The foundations are completed.
1924	April to Sept.	The steel frame is being assembled by McKinnon Steel Company of Sherbrooke. Foreman: M. Désilets.
1924	June 30	Granite cutting begins in a workshop set up in the Seminary yard. Foreman: Joseph Beaucage.
1924	September 14	Laying of the cornerstone.
1924	to 1931	Erection of the stone walls of the Basilica. Contractor and foreman: F.X. Lambert.
1929	July 26	The monumental statue is reinstalled on the gable.
1930	July 30	The pilgrims's bell is set up in the south tower.
1931	Spring	Granite laying is stopped. The towers are left unfinished.
1931	December 15	Copper sheet roofing work begins.
1933	October 18	Concrete casting of the crypt and the floor of the Basilica begins.
1934	April 24	The crypt is inaugurated.
1934	May 27	The Basilica is inaugurated by His Excellency, Martin Lajeunesse, Bishop of Keewatin.
1934	July	The miraculous statue is placed in the north part of the transept.
1934	July 26	The Basilica is officially inaugurated by His Eminence Cardinal Rodrigue Villeneuve.
1938	Feb. to June	Concrete casting of the central vault, the ambulatory and the radiating chapels: a surface of 27,500 square feet; 212 tons of concrete.
1940	February to July 1941	The central vault mosaic is completed by A. Labouret and J. Gaudin.

1942	June	Construction of the sacristy spiral stairs.
1943	to June 1944	Decoration of the crypt by Jos. Bernard and A. Labouret.
1945	Spring	Completion of the sacristy.
1945	May to July	The Holy Family chapel is completed.
1945	June to 1947	Carving of the frieze in the facade by Louis Parent of La Maîtrise d'Art de Montréal, with the help of Wilfrid Richard.
1945	December 16	His Excellency Bishop Georges Léon Pelletier blesses the new organ of the Basilica made by Casavant Co. of Saint-Hyacinthe.
1946	June 5	The Saint Joseph chapel is inaugurated by Father Marc Lussier.
1946	June 10	The chapel of Saint-Jean-Baptiste-de-la-Salle is inaugurated by Father Thomas Pelletier.
1946	July 25	Six bells are solemnly blessed by Archbishop Cushing of Boston.
1947	Winter and Spring	Completion of the chapels of the Great Relic, the Blessed Sacrement, St. Benedict, St. Joachim, St. Alphonsus, St. John the Baptizer, St. Patrick and St. Gerard.
194	November to Summer 1949	Completion of the sanctuary and the ambulatory. The materials are supplied by Martineau Co. and the work is supervised by Mr. Forest, engineer for Collet & Frères.
1949	April	Stained glass of Saint Ann of Jerusalem: A. Labouret.
1949	June	Stained glass of Saint Ann of Auray: A. Labouret.
1949	June	Émile Brunet's first capitals are translated into Indiana stone by Maurice Lord.
1949	November 19	Blessing of the crypt organ.
1950	Winter	The transept is completed.
1950	Winter	Stained glass panels in the sanctuary: rose windows and patriarchs.
1950	Spring	Wall mosaics in the sanctuary: A. Labouret.

1950	August 17	Silver tabernacle for the Blessed Sacrament altar: Albert Gilles of Cowansville.
1950	November to July 1951	Capitals in the sanctuary: Brunet and Lord.
1950	December to July 1951	The chapel of Our Lady of Perpetual Help is completed.
1953	to 1955 Winter seasons	Completion of the nave and aisles. Materials: Martineau Co.; foreman: Jean Coulombe.
1954	Winter	30 stained glass panels are installed: litany of the Saints and Beatitudes.
1957	March to May 1958	Construction of the outside steps of the Basilica.
1957	Fall	The facade is finished.
1958	March to May	Carving of the frieze of the Apostles by A. Marchetti.
1958	April 24	24 confessionals, made by Deslauriers Woodworks, are assembled.
1958	May 4	Blessing of three bells.
1958	November	Stained glass panels in the transept.
1959	February	The statues of the Evangelists are installed.
1959	Winter	The floors in the sanctuary and the ambulatory are finished. Communion rail and pulpit.
1960	February to April	Carving of the corner works on the pillars.
1961	January to April	34 stained glass panels are set up in the Clerestory; A. Labouret.
1961	June	Four statues are placed in the facade: the Virgin, St. Joachim, St. John the Baptizer, St. Joseph.
1962	January to April	Sanctuary stalls. Sculptor: Franz Moroder.
1962	March to October	The steeples are completed. Scaffoldings: Sarnia Co. Contractors: Dionne & Côté Co., Quebec.
1962	May to July	Main altar and Ciborium: Fabrico Co. of Montreal.
1962	May	Two statues in the facade: Mary of the Incarnation and Bishop de Laval.

20

1962	October 11	Setting up of the main altar-table.
1963	January to March	Carving of the inside tympanums over the doors: Brunet and Lord.
1963	March	Small stained glass windows in the aisles.
1964	March to May	Carving of the tympanums of the secondary altars: M. Lord.
1964	December to March	Setting up of the grilles in the sanctuary.
1965	January	Finishing work on the vestibule of the Basilica.
1965	January	Carving of the capitals in the aisles: L. Pagé.
1965	December	Bas-reliefs at the entrance. Sculptor: Hunter.
1966	February to May	Lighting system for the vaults.
1966	Spring and Fall	Mosaics of the 32 side vaults: Walter del Mistro.
1968-1971	Winter seasons	The pews are being installed. Sculpture: Franz Moroder. Woodwork: Nilus Leclerc, L'Isletville.
1968	October to May 1969	Paving of the floor of the Basilica.
1969	October to May 1970	Paving of the floor of the Basilica.
1975	May and September	Statues of the south porch in the facade: Kateri Mother d'Youville: Brunet and Lord.
1976	July 4	Consecration and dedication of the Basilica: Cardinal Maurice Roy.
1976	October	Statues of the north portal in the facade: Didace Pelletier and Alfred Pampalon: Brunet and Lord.
1977	March to May	Cleaning of the central vault and painting of the cement in which the mosaics are set: "Les Arts Religieux Appliqués" and Walter del Mistro.

B. THE FACADE OF THE BASILICA

In all, the facade makes up a rectangle of 160 feet by 300 feet. There are three vertical and three horizontal zones which

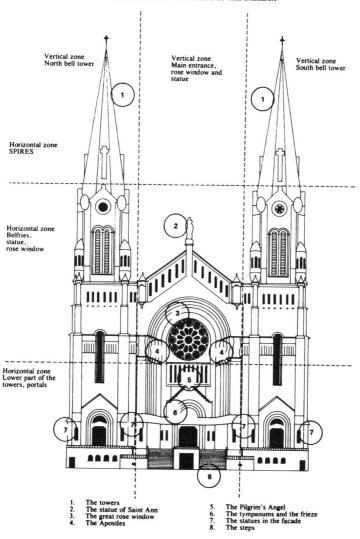

Vertical zone
North bell tower

Vertical zone
Main entrance,
rose window and
statue

Vertical zone
South bell tower

Horizontal zone
SPIRES

Horizontal zone
Belfries,
statue,
rose window

Horizontal zone
Lower part of the
towers, portals

1. The towers
2. The statue of Saint Ann
3. The great rose window
4. The Apostles

5. The Pilgrim's Angel
6. The tympanums and the frieze
7. The statues in the facade
8. The steps

spell harmony between the solids and voids in the facade. Here is what Father J.T. Nadeau wrote in the Annals of 1923 about the facade:

> "The facade corresponds to the nave and the two towers cover the aisles. From the bottom up, three portals, then the balcony surmounted by the great rose window matched with two long, narrow openings in the towers; still higher, an arcade alleviates the massiveness of the towers and brings out the inclines of the gable; finally, the belfries and the spires" (ABS, 1923, p. 203).

C. HIGHLIGHTS OF THE VARIOUS ELEMENTS IN THE FACADE:

1. THE SPIRES:

In 1931, construction work on the Basilica was stopped at the base of the spires. For 30 years, that is, from 1931 to 1962, the Basilica was seen with truncated towers. From March to October 1962, the spires were built by Côté & Dionne Co. of Quebec, with Carignan and Royer as engineers. With the crosses, the building now reaches to a height of 300 feet. The spires cap the towers:

> "At the height of the vast gable, the sturdy towers taper up as they rise with their Romanesque *corner turrets* and *twin splayed windows* flanked by slender shafts. They frame the gilt statue... Above the *belfries, crowned by four gables* pierced with *oculi,* will soar the octagonal spires". (J.T. Nadeau, priest, ABSA, 1923, p. 204)

2. THE STATUE OF SAINT ANN:

This statue had first been placed on the gable of the former Basilica. On March 29, 1922, when the fire destroyed this building, something unusual happened. Though made of wood and covered only with a thin sheet of copper, it did not burn when the steeples did. Moreover, the statue which had been braced to the roof with a copper bar, remained on the gable with the disconnected bar in the back, when the burning roof collapsed. Old parishioners said that a wooden peg had been put inside the base to keep the statue in place. But, when a crane lifted the statue to take it down, the workers were surprised to see that its base was imbedded only a few inches deep in the stone on

The front gable statue

After the first Basilica had been destroyed by the 1922 fire, the monumental statue of Saint Ann was exposed for veneration in the present square, in front of the Basilica then under construction. The above photograph was taken by Mary Coughlin, on July 26, 1929.

which it rested. This statue was made before the promulgation of a decree from Rome which would have authorized a crowned statue to be erected inside the church. That is why Saint Ann is represented here without a crown, in her role as teacher to the Virgin seated on her right arm.

This monumental sculpture was made in Gand, Belgium in 1885. When it was taken down from the gable in October, 1922, Brother Bruno Lizotte found, on the wood inside the base of the statue, a slip of paper with the following inscription: "Auguste Daurey ou Dhormy" "1885". (ASA, B-9b, 2/doc. 3350). According to ancient chronicles, it seems that C. Salières also might have worked on this statue. It is 13 feet, 6 inches high.

3. THE GREAT ROSE WINDOW:

The great rose is 23 feet in diameter and, as Father J.T. Nadeau said, it is somewhat "the logical center of the facade"

"Inscribed under the great arch voussoirs, flanked by the turrets and niches of the *tower buttresses,* the great rose blossoms into a tracery that is the logical center of the hole facade". (ABSA, 1923, p. 204)

4. THE APOSTLES:

In spring 1958, on the occasion of the tercentenary of Saint-Anne-de-Beaupré, the finishing touch was put on the facade when the still missing decorative columns and shafts were installed. At the same time, the *frieze of the Apostles* was carved. It spreads in two strips on either side of the rose window. Arnold Marchetti made the clay models of these twelve column-statues; they were then carved out of granite blocks by stone-cutters. Saint Peter makes up the recessed column on the right of the rose window; he holds his keys in his right hand and is slightly turned towards the Apostles to his left. Matching him, on the other side, is Saint Paul, the Apostles of the Gentilles; Saint Matthias does not appear in this frieze.

If you want to identify the Apostles in the sculptor's stone figures, please read the following diagram from left to right, that is, from north to south.

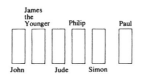

ROSE WINDOW

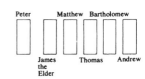

5. THE PILGRIM'S ANGEL:

The statue of the Pilgrim's Angel stands with its back against the stone cross topping the gable of the central porch. The design of this sculpture is the work of a Paris sculptor, André Vermare, who produced the model about 1926. While the facade was being finished and the frieze installed in 1957 and 1958, this statue was retouched in order to accentuate the folds of the drapery and to trim the silhouette of this angel, the Pilgrim's protector. He raises a blessing hand over the people coming in to pray.

6. THE TYMPANUM AND THE FRIEZE OF THE PILGRIMS:

The Church has three flaring out, *round arch portals,* with multiple rows of voussoirs and deep splays adorned with shafts and supporting sculptured archivolts nicely superposed and slightly receding one from the other. The three portals are linked together by the *frieze of the Pilgrims* and the central portal is decorated with a tympanum representing *Saint Ann as a "orante"*, that is, in a praying posture. As for the Pilgrim's Angel, André Vermare made the models of all the low-relief sculptures during the years 1925 and 1926. However, the overall arrangement of the scene was considerably altered when the frieze was carved by Louis Parent of "La Maîtrise d'Art de Montréal", with the help of Wilfrid Richard.

The praying figure of Saint Ann, in the tympanum, is flanked by four angels; at her feet, praying folks seem to be imploring the help of the powerful miracle-worker.

The frieze is a bas-relief inspired by History as well as by Canadian life.

South part, beginning *from the side of the river:*

Teachers, Canadian families, hospitals, farm life, evange-

26

lization of the Indians by the Jesuits, explorers, Bishop de Laval and Sir de Tracy.

North part, beginning *from the side of the hill:*

People of various walks of life come in procession to pray Saint Ann: a construction worker at the Basilica, its chief architect, L.-N. Audet, clergymen, Christian women, soldiers, sailors and a Bishop leading the procession. The procession stops beside a boat from which seamen disembark to thank Saint Ann for her protection in time of danger. The scene next to the central tympanum, represents the proclamation by Pope Leo XIII of the decree elevating Saint Ann's church to the status of a Basilica; in the background, can be seen the facade of the old Basilica, which a magnificent oak tree links to the main scene...

7. THE FACADE STATUES:

In the lower part of the tower buttresses and in the spaces on either side of the central porch colonnade, there are niches containing statues carved in Indiana stone. Émile Brunet made the clay models of these statues and Maurice Lord carved them. On the north and south side tower buttresses, there are also four other statues that one can see while climbing the side steps.

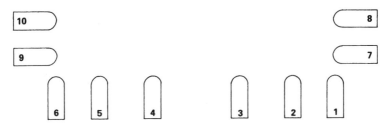

The four central statues, namely Saint Joachim (2), the Holy Virgin (3), Saint Joseph (4) and Saint John the Baptizer (5) were installed in June 1961: the statues of Mary of the Incarnation (1) and of Bishop de Laval (6) were put in place in May 1962, but in the reverse order; in October 1976, they were removed and placed in the order they are now. The statues of Kateri Tekakwita (7) and of Marguerite d'Youville (8) were placed in their niches, the former in May, the latter in September 1975. Finally, in October 1976, the statues of Father Pampalon (9) and of Brother Didace Pelletier (10) were hoisted into their niches. These are the last works of sculptor Émile Brunet, who died in February 1977. Here is a word on each of these statues to help discover the sculptor's intention.

1. Mary of the Incarnation:

Venerable Mary of the Incarnation, who founded the Ursulines of Quebec, wrote to her son on September 30, 1665:

"At seven leagues from here, there is a town called Petit-Cap where stands a church dedicated to Saint Ann in which Our Lord works wonders on behalf of the Blessed Virgin's Mother". (Letters, tome 2, p. 310)

On the right arm of the statue, rests a tiny church as a reminder of both the small church of Petit-Cap and Saint Ann' chapel, which the Venerable had intended to build and which was erected by Sir de Tracy.

2. Saint Joachim:

He is the Blessed Virgin's father and Saint Ann's husband. Brunet has represented him on the way back from his vineyard. A vine-plant appears at his feet and his hands cradle a dove symbolizing his priestly function at the temple.

3. Mary, the Blessed Virgin:

She is Saint Ann's daughter and the mother of Jesus. The artist was bent on representing her as the *Mother of God,* holding her well-swaddled Jesus in her hands. According to Brunet's idea, the dove in the Child's hands is a wooden toy, made for him by Saint Joseph.

4. Saint Joseph:

Brunet wanted Saint Joseph to appear young, vigorous and full of joy. As a carpenter, the saint holds a tool and a piece of wood, which, judging from the shavings at his feet, he has just planed.

5. Saint John the Baptizer:

As Christ's Precursor and French Canadians' Patron saint, he deserved a choice place. Brunet envisioned him as a prophet, his body emaciated by fasting and his face beaming with inspiration.

He lived in the desert as is indicated by the cactuses on the base, but here he is draped in the ample robe of a prophet.

6. Bishop de Laval:

He was Quebec's first Bishop and nurtured a deep affection for Saint Ann and her shrine in Beaupré. On June 25, 1680, he wrote:

> "Nothing has helped us more efficiently to bear the pastoral burden of this nascent Church than the special devotion which all the inhabitants of this country show to Saint Ann..."

This very sentence inspired the artist. The Bishop is shown holding in one hand a book containing his episcopal mandates. With the other hand, he points to a maple seedling while holding a scroll on which are written the words: "Ego plantavi", "I have planted". These words of Saint Paul, summing up the Apostle's work in the Church, are used here to recall the implantation of the Canadian Church, symbolized by the maple seedling.

7. Kateri Tekakwita:

The Indians have always shown over the years a tender devotion to Saint Ann. It was only suitable to recall this age-old fidelity by placing, in one of the niches, the Iroquois Virgin of Caughnawaga. Brunet has represented her in Indian clothes and absorbed in prayer.

8. Blessed Marguerite d'Youville:

She lived in Varennes, a place dedicated to Saint Ann, where people still venerate a miraculous painting crowned by

Bishop de Laval, Quebec's first Bishop
The impressive figure of the first pastor of the Church of Quebec as it appears
in one of the niches of the Basilica. Émile Brunet made the clay model which
Maurice Lord translated into Indiana stone. (Photograph by Camil Lesieur)

Bust of Kateri Tekakwita

This photograph is that of the clay model by sculptor Maurice Lord to carve the statue in the south niche. This piece typifies the work of Émile Brunet, who created the statues of the Sainte-Anne-de-Beaupré Basilica. (Photograph by Philippe H. Laporte)

Bishop Bourget. Mother d'Youville, foundress of the Sisters of Charity, is shown here handing out bread; she has three buns in her hand and at her feet there is a basketful of bread.

9. Father Alfred Pampalon C.Ss.R.:

Father Pampalon was a young Redemptorist priest who died about the end of the last century and whose case for beatification has been introduced in the Roman Catholic Court. His remains are preserved in the crypt of the Basilica. He died in the prime of life, sapped by tuberculosis. Brunet envisioned him slightly stooped, like a consumptive, and holding a book inscribed with the monogram of the Blessed Virgin, to whom he was tenderly devoted.

10. Brother Didace Pelletier, O.F.M.:

Brother Didace Pelletier, whose real name was Claude Pelletier, was baptized at Sainte-Anne in 1657, by Father André Richard, a Jesuit. While he was a Recollet, he was widely known as a holy man. Since he was a carpenter, he is represented at work but, as it were, momentarily absorbed in some peaceful reflexion. Besides, he is slightly turned toward the farm that his father, Georges Pelletier, Saint-Anne's first sacristan, owned on top of the hill on the east side. On that hill, stands also a monument to the memory of Brother Didace.

8. THE STEPS OF THE BASILICA:

It was not before 1957 that the steps leading to the Basilica were built. Work on these steps, 276 feet wide, lasted from March 1957 to May 1958. Four granite stairs, two on the sides and two in the front, 86 steps in all, lead to the parvis so paved as to facilitate water drainage. There are also two ramps for wheel-chairs.

Under the steps are located some of the *Reception Desks,* where Fathers and Brothers stay all year long to help visitors with information or administrative services: subscription to the magazine, Mass offering and the like... Facing the reception desks, are the quarters of *Saint Ann's Aides,* who seasonally serve lame and sick pilgrims. Saint Ann's Aides have been organized in a volunteer sodality or confraternity since 1949.

9. THE BELLS OF THE BASILICA:

The chimes of the Basilica comprise nine bells of which six are in the south tower and three, the heavier ones, in the north tower. The first six were blessed on July 25, 1946, by Archbishop Cushing of Boston and inaugurated the same year on the 22nd of September. The last three bells were blessed on May 4, 1958; their names are "Angelica", "Jesus", and "Mary". The total weight of the nine bells amounts to 43,087 pounds, nearly 22 tons.

Among these bells, one has its own story. It is the *Pilgrim's great bells,* which was rehoisted into the south tower on July 30, 1930. This bell had first been placed in the belfry of the old Basilica and had fallen down when the belfry collapsed in the fire of 1922. Then, it had been used again in the belfry of the temporary church until, a year later, it cracked and had to be returned to Europe for recasting. In 1924, it was brought back and reinstalled in the belfry of the temporary church, but it was so badly damaged in the burning of the chapel in 1926, that it had to be recast in Europe again.

Here is the complete list of the bells of the Basilica:

Name	Tone	Weight (in pounds)
Angelica	sol	11,936
Jesus	la	8,427
Mary	si	6,074
Ann	do	5,450
Joachim	ré	4,000
Joseph	mi	2,500
John the Baptizer	fa	2,100
Alphonsus	sol	1,550
Patrick	la	1,050

3. THE NARTHEX OR VESTIBULE OF THE BASILICA

(We suggest now that you climb the front steps or the ramps to enter the Basilica through the central door. Let us stop a while to examine the vestibule.)

1. COMPLETION OF THE VESTIBULE:

The vestibule was completed during the 1964-1965 winter season. Louis-N. Audet, chief architect of the Basilica, drew the plans and supervised the work, requiring the professional services of many artists for the sculptures and the mosaics. Sculpting was assigned to Hunter and to Clément Paré, then director of "École des Beaux Arts" in Quebec; they carved the capitals and the bas-reliefs. The stone of the walls and of the columns comes from Saint-Marc-des-Carrières and the black granite of the plinths, from Rivière-à-Pierre.

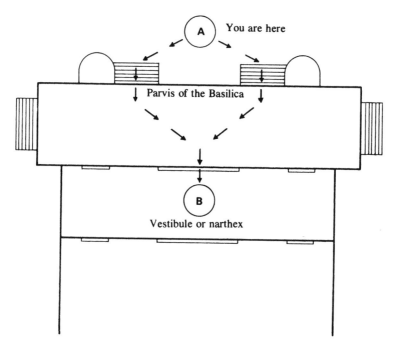

The main ornament of the vestibule is the *mosaic decoration* on the vaults, on part of the walls and on the floor. The entire mosaic work was executed by Walter del Mistro. He had already worked at the Basilica since the beginning of such work.

2. THE MAIN IDEA BEHIND THE VESTIBULE DECORATION

This decoration is meant to evoke *the human being's world* as it emerged *from the Creator's hands* and as it is *transformed by man's activity.* The evocation brings out the profound meaning of the world as an homage to God.

> "All the decoration of the vestibule was conceived as a vast ensemble, a lavish presentation of the Creator's work in the Universe, a work continued by man, his creature". (Laurent Proulx, C.Ss.R. Les voûtes secondaires, p. 8)

To those who would like a more elaborate visit of the vestibule, we suggest two books available at the information center. They reveal the profound meaning of the symbols represented in the mosaics and the sculptures. Please, refer to:

Laurent Proulx, C.Ss.R., **"The Mosaic Pavements of Saint Ann's Basilica"**. An explanation of the narthex pavement will be found on pages 2 to 7.

Laurent Proulx, C.Ss.R., **"Les voûtes secondaires de la Basilique"**. The vestibule vaults are explained on pages 8 to 21.

3. BRIEF DESCRIPTION OF THE VESTIBULE DECORATION:

A. Evocation of Time: the day, months, seasons.

The day is *graphically* pictured on the vault near the central door by a circle, which divides in two halves, one gold, the other dark blue: the former stands for daytime, the latter for nightime. Moreover, the 24 hours of the day are inscribed all around the circle.

The *seasons,* appear on the bases of the small central vaults: spring, summer, autumn and winter are each symbolized by a female figure on an appropriate background.

The *months* are represented by the zodiac signs in the tympanums of the cradle-shaped sections of the walls. The whole astronomical bestiary, inherited from ancient Chaldea, is displayed here:

March:	Aries, the Ram	September:	Libra, the Balance
April:	Taurus, the Bull	October:	Scorpio, the Scorpion
May:	Gemini, the Twins	November:	Sagittarius, the Archer
June:	Cancer, the Crab	December:	Capricorn, the Goat
July:	Leo, the Lion	January:	Aquarius, the Water Bearer
August:	Virgo, the Virgin	February:	Pisces, the fishes

b. Evocation of Life and Death:

All the vaults are covered with pictures of flowers, birds, fishes, beasts, plants and fruits. It is a vast synthesis of life in God's creation. The bright colors of the mosaic are set off by a network of fine gold lines.

The decoration of the capitals was inspired by the North American flora: the maple, the oak, the pine, the fir, the birch, the hemlock, the poplar, etc.

The two *chapels* at either end of the narthex evoke life and death. On the north side is the baptistry where we are born to eternal life through the action of water and the Holy Spirit. Behind the grille whose door is decorated with two fishes, you can see a large white Carrara marble basin adorned with a "round of the new born", expressing the exuberant joy of the new life emerging from the baptismal waters. The mosaics of the baptistry chapel recall Gospel scenes related to Baptism: Jesus' Baptism, the Resurrection, the Pentecost.

Facing this chapel, at the east of the narthex, is the *Calvary chapel.* It reminds us how death was defeated by the Lord and changed into a passage to eternal life. On either side of the white marble Calvary, there are six panels concealing the reliquaries in which are kept relics of martyrs: namely, believers who faced death rather than give up their faith in the Lord and who entered eternal life by giving the blood testimony.

The *dance of life:* The *fleeting nature of life* is pictured in the rectangle flooring before the central door. The symbolical figures of a man and a woman dancing to the beat of a tambourine represent the *"joy of living",* but a joy that is as short-lived as a dance movement.

c. Evocation of Human Activities:

These are pictured in the mosaic flooring and in two different ways. In the *quadrilaterals,* are shown various *crafts* of man:

On the north side: farm life, blacksmithing, baking, carpentry.

On the south side: lumbering, shore coasting, office work, masonry.

In the *two ornamental circles* near the secondary doors, the following are shown by means of symbolical figures surrounded by appropriate attributes:

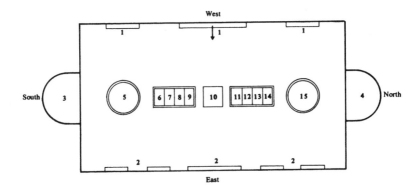

The Vestibule Floor of the Basilica

1. Outside doors of the vestibule
2. Inside doors of the vestibule
3. Calvary chapel
4. Baptistry
5. Symbolic figure: the Sciences
6. Lumbering
7. Shore coasting
8. Office work
9. Masonry
10. Dance
11. Carpentry
12. Baking
13. Blacksmithing
14. Farm work
15. Symbolic figure: the Arts

Northside: The Arts: Painting, Music, Drama, Architecture, Sculpture, Ceramics.

Southside: The Sciences: Geography, Geodesy, Astronomy, Chemistry, Biology, Modern Balistics.

d. The Bas-Reliefs of the Main Entrance:

The bas-reliefs were carved in December 1965 by Hunter, then teacher at l'École des Beaux Arts in Quebec. They represent two great transformations which take place here at Saint-Anne-de-Beaupré: *spiritual conversion and physical cure.*

Northside Bas-relief: Conversion

This carving was inspired by the following text from Saint Matthew (5, 23-24):

"If you bring your gift to the altar and, there, recall that your brother has anything against you, leave your gift at the altar, go first to be reconciled with your brother and then come and offer your gift".

Southside Bas-relief: Cure of a Cripple.

This bas-relief is meant to illustrate what is said in Acts (3, 6-8): The Apostles Peter and John met a cripple at the Beautiful Gate of the Temple and the cripple begged them for an alm. Peter said:

"I have neither silver nor gold, but what I have I give you! In the name of Jesus Christ the Nazarean, walk! Then Peter took him by the right hand and pulled him up. Immediately the beggar's feet and ankles became strong; he jumped up, stood for a moment, then began to walk around. He went into the Temple with them — walking, jumping about and praising God".

4. THE GREAT NAVE

(For this visit of the Basilica, we suggest that you enter through the central door of the facade. You will then be facing the nave. If you stop somewhere behind the pews, at the back of the church, you will be at the right spot to begin your visit.)

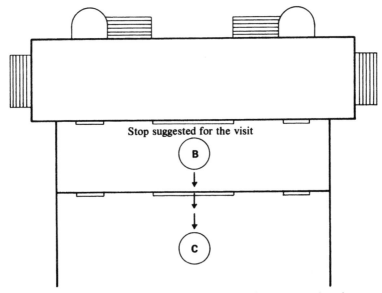

Stop suggested for the visit

B

C

1. General information to be read before you begin your detailed visit of the Basilica.

A. The **Ex-Votos** on **the two Pillars** near the Church Entrance.

One of the things you notice as soon as you enter the Basilica, is the display of hundreds of crutches, walking-sticks and prostheses fixed to the two pillars at the entrance of the church. They are ex-votos, that is, objects placed there as a token of gratitude for the favor of a cure. It is important to understand, at the onset of your visit, that the Shrine of Sainte-Anne-de-Beaupré *is not just a parochial church,* but a place of pilgrimage. One reason which, for three centuries, has justified the vocation of this place of prayer, is an uninterrupted series of special divine interventions on behalf of the sick and cripples through Saint Ann's intercession.

It all began in 1658. French Canada's population was then little more than one thousand inhabitants. There were churches available for worship to people in the parishes of Quebec, Three-Rivers and Montreal. Quebec's parish-priest, Thubières of Queylus, on a pastoral visit to the Beaupré hill, realized that two more churches had to be built for the people of the neighborhood.

One church would minister to the territory between Montmorency River and Rivière-aux-Chiens and would be dedicated to Mary; it is now the parish next to Château-Richer. At the same time, it was decided that another church would minister to the territory between Rivière-aux-Chiens and Great-River (now called Saint Ann's River); this church would be dedicated to Saint Ann, Mother of Mary, Grandmother of Jesus. Étienne de Lessard presented Sir Thubières de Queylus with a plot of land on March 8, 1658 and, as was said before, Father Vignal accompanied by Governor d'Ailleboust, blessed the future site of the church on March 13, 1658. In spring, when work started on the foundations of the chapel, a cripple, Louis Guimond, who lived in Petit-Cap, took trouble to come and, out of devotion, he laid three stones in the foundations. He was cured on the spot. This cure was followed by many others in subsequent years. So, the first parish-priest of Sainte-Anne-du-Petit-Cap (that was Sainte-Anne-de-Beaupré's name at the time) wrote a narrative of the "marvels" worked through Saint Ann's intercession. This narrative was included in the Jesuits' Relations. Bishop de Laval, the country's first Bishop himself gave credit to this narrative. Such interventions have never stopped ever since.

Many terms have been used by those who have related these facts; they spoke of "wonders", "miracles", "cures", "favors" to qualify a *change* often quick or sudden in the state of health of a sick person then considered incurable. And, in every case, this change came with *an act of devotion of some kind:* a pilgrimage, a novena, veneration of Saint Ann's relic, private or group prayers, etc. The Custodians of the Shrine, while respecting the testimony of those reporting a cure, investigate further and require *two certificates from the doctor.* One describes the state of the health *before the cure;* the second is a statement on the state of health *after the reported intervention.*

The ex-votos fixed to the pillars are only a small number of the crutches and prostheses of all kinds left here by grateful pilgrims. During the 1922 fire, many such objects were burned with the church, and have not been replaced by other ones on the pillars. But, what is important to remember is that all these things were given up by people who needed them before Saint Ann' intercession and who have asked that the objets be exposed at the Shrine as tokens of gratitude for their cure. On the second floor of the Museum, there are also ex-votos to be seen. Those are older and date back to the beginnings of the country: votive paintings and various objects of another age.

B. General presentation of the interior of the Basilica:

Louis-N. Audet, one of the architects of the Basilica, presents it as a "five-nave church with a sanctuary and absidial chapels". The idea to build a five-nave (one nave and four aisles) church was apparently inspired by the cathedral of Bourges, France. And the architects' first intention was to build a "*vast* church, *Gothic* in its proportions, but *Romanesque* in its details" (ABSA 1950, p. 342). The Romanesque style was then little known in Canada, but had begun to make its way under the influence of Richardson in English-speaking Canada and in the United States.

The interior of the church has changed over the years. Before 1954, it was nothing but bare walls with visible steel structures pertaining to the *metal framework* erected in April 1924, by McKinnon Steel Co. of Sherbrooke under the supervision of foreman M. Desilets. The bulk of the metal framework weighs *898 tons.* Maintenance workers who have access to the attic above the vault of the Basilica, such as electricians, and lighting or acoustics experts, have a chance to marvel at this sturdy metal framework erected more than 50 years ago.

In 1938, the central vault, the ambulatory and the side-chapels were cast, adding a weight of 212 tons of concrete. Between 1947 and 1954, the entire surface of the walls and columns was covered with stone, namely with 31 040 blocks of stone, an additional weight of 4 343 tons. To this weight of about 5 000 tons, other additions were made later, but in smaller quantities. Now, if you add to this mass the total weight of the granite in the exterior walls, you can imagine how firm the foundations of the Basilica of Sainte-Anne-de-Beaupré must be.

C. The interior parts

For the detailed visit of the church, it is useful to know how the interior space of the Basilica is divided.

The interior of the Basilica in 1932
This old photograph gives a good idea of what the interior of the Basilica looked like before the steel structure was covered with stone. (Photograph by Brother Jacques Naud)

1. The Nave and the Aisles

The nave:	45 feet wide (13,7 metres)
	85 feet high (25,9 metres)
The inner aisles:	18 feet wide (5,4 metres)
	45 feet high (13,7 metres)
The outer aisles:	18 feet wide (5,4 metres)
	20 feet high (6,09 metres)

The nave is bordered by pillars and columns that support the central vault and part of the inner aisles thrust; the outer aisles are furnished with pilasters. The total width of the main body is *135 feet* or 41,1 metres.

2. The Transept: The church construction follows the general design of a Latin cross. The transept is that part of the church which stands at right angle with the nave and links it with the sanctuary. The transept is 200 feet long or 60,9 metres and 45 feet wide, that is, the same width as the nave. It is in the north end of the transept that you find what some people like to call the "shrine". That is where Saint Ann's miraculous statue stands, together with the Chapel of the Great Relic.

3. The Sanctuary: It is 45 feet wide and extends from the transept to a maximum length of 65 feet or 19,6 metres.

4. The Apse: Around the sanctuary, runs an ambulatory surrounded by radiating chapels.

5. The Choir Loft: The choir loft above the vestibule of the Basilica, contains the grand organ and the great rose window of the facade.

The Basilica has a seating capacity of 1 500 people, that is, 1 372 in the nave and aisles, and 123 in the sanctuary.

2. DETAILED VISIT OF THE INTERIOR: THE NAVE AND THE AISLES

(For the detailed visit of the Basilica, a very simple course is

suggested: the explanations on the nave and the aisles may well be read at the entrance. So as to be methodical, our description will proceed from top to bottom, that is from the vault to the floor. And the explanations will always call your attention first to the north side of the church, the side of the hill, on your left. However, there will be no question of sides when we give explanations referring to a certain type of decoration extending to the entire church, as is the case with mosaics, stained glass windows, sculptures...)

1. THE MOSAICS OF THE CENTRAL VAULT

An elaborate description of the central vault is given in a booklet by Father Laurent Proulx, C.Ss.R., The title is "The Central Arch in the Basilica of Sainte-Anne-de-Beaupré", 1977, about 70 pages. Here are only a few brief observations.

The builders of the Basilica had first intended the vaulting to be a system of groined vaults. But, in 1937, a different design was adopted: a *long barrel vault* with a few transverse ribs and terminated by a half-cupola. From February to June 1938, the concrete was cast. Altogether, 550 tons of Haydite or pumice stone, mixed with 212 tons or 5 100 sacks of cement, produced a 27 500 square-foot surface to be decorated.

Mosaic was chosen as the means of decoration. Not all the surface, but half of it, was covered with mosaic; only the scenes, figures and inscriptions were to be represented in ceramic or with gilt pieces embedded in cement. In 1977, when the central vault was cleaned, the cement was coated with acrylic, salmon-color paint. The mosaic work was executed during the years 1940 and 1941; 37 years later, thanks to the paint on the background cement, the central vault began to glisten with the pervading bright tone that can be observed today. This finishing touch had been purposely delayed until the completion of the stone covering and the stained glass windows in order to choose, for the vault, the background color that would best harmonize with the general tone of the church.

The mosaic decoration work was commissioned to two Paris artists, *Jean Gaudin and Auguste Labouret*. The basic work was done in a Paris workshop. After the entire decoration program had been agreed upon, large quantities of precision-cut bits of glass and ceramic were assembled on full-scale sketches. Then, a sheet of strong paper was glued on the face to be exposed to view; all the pieces of this giant puzzle were carefully numbered before being shipped in cases to Sainte-Anne-de-Beaupré. Meanwhile, the vault had been prepared for the laying. First of all, the entire decoration surface was striated, that is, grooves were scratched into the cement so as to give grip to the coating. Then the numbered pieces were properly reassembled. And, after the coating had sufficiently set, the paper was soaked with water and removed. The finishing job consisted in neatly filling the cracks between the pieces.

The theme of the central vault decoration is *the life of Saint Ann* to whom the church is dedicated. The 26 biographic scenes derive from a narrative in Saint James' Protogospel, a second-century book, containing the traditional life story of the Mother of Mary and Grandmother of Jesus. To Saint Ann's earthly life, were added, in the transept and the sanctuary, two symbolic scenes depicting *Saint Ann's virtues and her glorification in Heaven.* In short, one should bear in mind that the entire ceiling surface of the nave, the transept and the sanctuary makes up a vast decorative ensemble representing Saint Ann's life; *her earthly life* in the nave, *her virtues* in the transept and *her heavenly glorification* in the sanctuary. The different scenes of Saint Ann's life can easily be identified with the help of the diagram herewith.

The essential function of mosaic decoration is precisely to decorate an architectural structure. The basic idea is that *the decoration must conform to the architecture* of the building. The decorator must respect the architectural forms of the building he is decorating and must make sure there is visible unity in his work. Moreover, because of the distance from which his work is to be seen, in this case 85 feet, the mosaic artist must imagine everything on the proper scale: the size of the figures, the relative proportions of the decorative elements, the legibility of the inscriptions, etc. Respect for the architectural values also dictates the *choice of color.* The colors must be moderate but well set off against a clear background. Here the back-

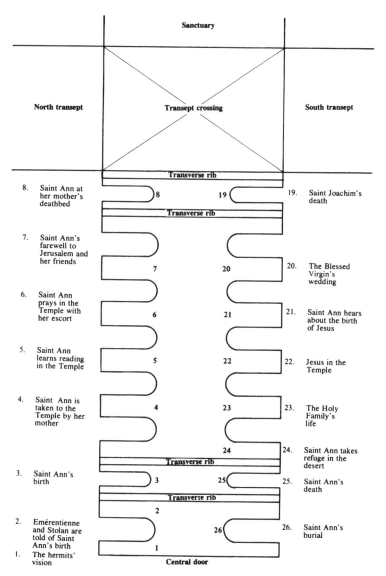

Sanctuary

North transept | Transept crossing | South transept

Transverse rib

8. Saint Ann at her mother's deathbed

8   19   19. Saint Joachim's death

Transverse rib

7. Saint Ann's farewell to Jerusalem and her friends

7   20   20. The Blessed Virgin's wedding

6. Saint Ann prays in the Temple with her escort

6   21   21. Saint Ann hears about the birth of Jesus

5. Saint Ann learns reading in the Temple

5   22   22. Jesus in the Temple

4. Saint Ann is taken to the Temple by her mother

4   23   23. The Holy Family's life

24   24. Saint Ann takes refuge in the desert

Transverse rib

3. Saint Ann's birth

3   25   25. Saint Ann's death

Transverse rib

2

2. Emérentienne and Stolan are told of Saint Ann's birth

26   26. Saint Ann's burial

1. The hermits' vision

1

Central door

THE MOSAICS IN THE NAVE

ground resembles an ocherbrown carpet touched up with red and gold. The gold however is not applied in large masses, but forms a sort of discreet and pervading network, so arranged as to make the vault sparkle in harmony with the changing light that illuminates it.

2. THE TRIFORIUM:

Under the vault, there is a strip of architectural decoration called the *"triforium"*. It is a gallery extending all around the church, above the arches of the columns and pillars, and forming a luminous decoration in the upper part of the nave, of the transept and the sanctuary. The architects, Audet and Roisin, exerted considerable effort on this clerestory ornament. For a long time, it was debated whether the triforium should materialize into a *number of separate bays* or into a *continuous decoration*. Finally, a compromise solution was adopted: separate bays in the nave and the transept; in the sanctuary, narrower bays, but so close to one another as to give the illusion of continuity. The openings of this gallery are flanked by twin columns topped by one and the same elaborately carved capital. All the ornamental motifs of the capitals differ from one another. Despite their great number, not one motif is repeated.

The triforium columns are carved in marble of different colors. The visitor will be able to identify the different kinds of marble more easily by observing similar columns at close range in the chapels of the ambulatory when his detailed visit takes him there.

There are *326 marble columns* in the triforium, namely:

In the nave:
10 bays with 10 columns each = 100 columns
4 bays with 8 columns each = 32 columns
a total of 132 columns in the nave.

In the transept:
8 bays with 10 columns each = 80 columns
4 bays with 8 columns = 32 columns
a total of 112 columns in the transept.

In the sanctuary:
11 bays with 6 columns each =   66 columns
2 bays with 8 columns each =   16 columns
                         a total of 82 columns in the sanctuary.

While looking at the triforium, it is easy to concentrate on certain architectural details of the Basilica. For instance, one can notice that there are *balustrades* added to the triforium decoration at both ends of the transverse ribs. Now, let us say a word about the finish stone of the church. The transverse ribs and the cornice that borders the central vault are of *Indiana stone*. As for the finish stone of the wall between the cornice and the triforium arcade, it is the kind used for the finish everywhere else in the Basilica. It is a cream color stone, porous enough to be of high acoustic quality; it is *Texas Travertine* commonly called "Cordova".

Under the cornice bordering the vault, there are inscriptions in golden letters. They express *litany invocations* to Saint Ann and verses of *traditional hymns* regularly sung at pilgrimage celebrations. The inscription below the north cornice was taken from a hymn rarely sung today, but very popular at the time the Basilica was decorated:

"Saint Ann, O Good Saint Ann,   O teach us to be Christians,
Here come thy children dear.   Our prayers kindly hear".

On the south wall of the nave, is inscribed the second part of a hymn refrain which is more than 110 years old. The hymn "All Hail Saint Ann" was heard for the first time here in 1887, when the Montreal "Congréganistes", led by composer M. Martineau, a Sulpician, sang it on entering the Shrine. The first part of the refrain is inscribed on the west wall of the south transept; on the south wall of the nave, the first words of the refrain have been repeated and the last part has been inscribed below.

"All hail Saint Ann, our great and mighty Patron, Beloved by God, she hearkens to our prayer".

3. THE CAPITALS OF THE COLUMNS AND THE CORNER SCULPTURES OF THE PILLARS

The triforium arches rest on columns and pillars. In the

nave, there are eight columns, four on each side. There are also four pillars in the front and two pillars in the back completed by two half-pillars supporting arches and the wall of the choir loft. These columns and pillars are crowned with sculptures; the columns have *capitals with historic motifs* and the pillars are decorated at the top with *symbolic corner sculptures*. All these sculptures were executed by two artists who worked together for a long time in the Basilica. *Émile Brunet* made the clay models of the capitals and the corner sculptures; *Maurice Lord* translated Brunet's creations into stone, striving to express the subtle meaning of the lines and all the intended light and shadow effects, in the proper language of his material. Brunet is responsible for the original idea, the very creation of the work. To Lord goes credit for the masterful treatment of the blond Indiana stone in which the capitals and corner motifs were carved.

a. The Capitals of the Columns:

The capitals of the Basilica are made up of 2 stone blocks weighing three tons altogether. The sculpture covers the four faces of the capital; each face is 5 feet by 5 1/4 feet. The relief is a maximum of 8 inches thick. "A novelty in this country: these capitals represent historic scenes; the theme is the life of Christ". (Louis-N. Audet, ASA, B-10a, b.14/doc. 17 781, p. 10).

It had been decided that Saint Ann's Basilica should have its *"stone Gospel"* as was the custom with Romanesque churches. The project was easily feasible, since there were 88 stone slabs to be carved. This stone Gospel relates the mysteries of *Jesus' infancy* (sanctuary), his miracles and his parables. In the nave, the north side, that is, the whole system of capitals on the side of the hill, represents the *glorious mysteries:* the Resurrection, the Ascension, the Pentecost, etc... the south side evokes the *sorrowful mysteries* of the passion and death of Jesus. To see how the scenes have been distributed on each capital and each corner member, please refer to the diagram herewith.

The technique used here is quite simple: the idea is, above all, to safeguard the architectural function of the capital, which is to crown a column and to artistically link a round column to a square slab above it. The artistic principle is easily detected:

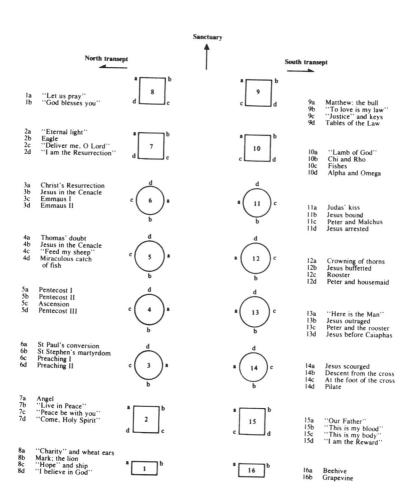

Sanctuary

North transept

South transept

1a	"Let us pray"	
1b	"God blesses you"	

8

9	
9a	Matthew: the bull
9b	"To love is my law"
9c	"Justice" and keys
9d	Tables of the Law

2a	"Eternal light"	
2b	Eagle	
2c	"Deliver me, O Lord"	
2d	"I am the Resurrection"	

7

10

10a	"Lamb of God"
10b	Chi and Rho
10c	Fishes
10d	Alpha and Omega

3a	Christ's Resurrection	
3b	Jesus in the Cenacle	
3c	Emmaus I	
3d	Emmaus II	

6

11

11a	Judas' kiss
11b	Jesus bound
11c	Peter and Malchus
11d	Jesus arrested

4a	Thomas' doubt	
4b	Jesus in the Cenacle	
4c	"Feed my sheep"	
4d	Miraculous catch of fish	

5

12

12a	Crowning of thorns
12b	Jesus buffetted
12c	Rooster
12d	Peter and housemaid

5a	Pentecost I	
5b	Pentecost II	
5c	Ascension	
5d	Pentecost III	

4

13

13a	"Here is the Man"
13b	Jesus outraged
13c	Peter and the rooster
13d	Jesus before Caiaphas

6a	St Paul's conversion	
6b	St Stephen's martyrdom	
6c	Preaching I	
6d	Preaching II	

3

14

14a	Jesus scourged
14b	Descent from the cross
14c	At the foot of the cross
14d	Pilate

7a	Angel	
7b	"Live in Peace"	
7c	"Peace be with you"	
7d	"Come, Holy Spirit"	

2

15

15a	"Our Father"
15b	"This is my blood"
15c	"This is my body"
15d	"I am the Reward"

8a	"Charity" and wheat ears	
8b	Mark; the lion	
8c	"Hope" and ship	
8d	"I believe in God"	

1

16

16a	Beehive
16b	Grapevine

**Subjects of the sculptures on the capitals of the columns
and the upper corners of the pillars in the nave**

human figures are privileged, with little attention to decoration and background. The artist is satisfied with harmonizing very simple lines: arm and leg movement, graceful drapery and emphasis on face expression, all of which point to the childlike simplicity of the artist that was Émile Brunet. He illustrated Our Lord's life with tender feeling. Maurice Lord, an expert in stone carving, managed, through extremely varied incisions, to discreetly turn the stone blocks into surfaces that grip light or shadow ... smooth parts, rough parts, striated or fluted with chisels and gouges, where light dances subtly all around the capital.

b. The Corner Sculptures of the Pillars:

The massive pillars at the rear of the nave and at the transept crossing, are not crowned with capitals, but decorated at their upper corners with carved motifs called "corner works" or "corner sculptures". The technique used in the nave was the same as that used for the capitals; those in the sanctuary result from a different technique: a kind of lacework in very low relief as a simple decoration. The overall decoration program for the corner sculptures is also more simple. In the nave and the transept, each pillar is decorated with a group of symbols expressing one particular theme. All the themes refer to Liturgy. If you look at the diagram identifying the decorative subjects chosen for the nave, you will realize that the north rear pillar evokes the idea of death and the south one, the *Eucharistic Mystery.*

4. THE STAINED GLASS WINDOWS IN THE NAVE:

In the nave of the Basilica, there are 63 stained glass windows; altogether, the church has *240 stained glass windows.* For nearly all of these, a new technique has been used, namely, *thick glass set in concrete.* 214 stained glass windows were executed in this way: the remaining 26 windows, which are in the ambulatory, consist of relatively thin glass set in lead strips. All the panels of thick, concrete-set glass were produced at *Auguste Labouret's* Paris workshop. He was assisted by stained glass expert *Pierre Chaudière.* The idea behind these windows

STAINED GLASS WINDOWS IN THE NAVE: NORTH SIDE

A. The Clerestory Stained Glass Windows: Triplets and Bull's-Eyes

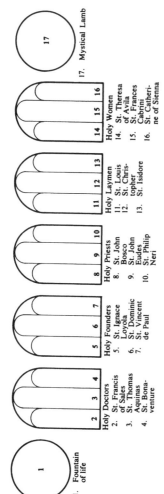

1. Fountain of life

Holy Doctors
2. St. Francis of Sales
3. St. Thomas Aquinas
4. St. Bonaventure

Holy Founders
5. St. Ignace Loyola
6. St. Dominic
7. St. Vincent de Paul

Holy Priests
8. St. John Bosco
9. St. John Eudes
10. St. Philip Neri

Holy Laymen
11. St. Louis
12. St. Christopher
13. St. Isidore

Holy Women
14. St. Theresa of Avila
15. St. Frances Cabrini
16. St. Catherine of Sienna

17. Mystical Lamb

B. The Inner Aisle stained glass Windows: twin windows

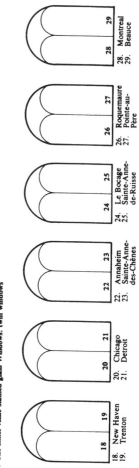

18. New Haven
19. Trenton

20. Chicago
21. Detroit

22. Annaheim
23. Sainte-Anne-des-Chênes

24. Le Bocage
25. Sainte-Anne-de-Ruisse

26. Roquemaure
27. Pointe-au-Père

28. Montreal
29. Beauce

STAINED GLASS WINDOWS IN THE NAVE: SOUTH SIDE

A. The Clerestory Stained Glass Windows: triplets and Bull's-Eyes

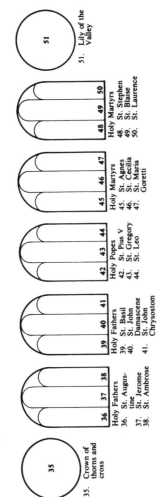

35. Crown of thorns and cross

Holy Fathers
36. St. Augustine
37. St. Jerome
38. St. Ambrose

Holy Fathers
39. St. Basil
40. St. John Damascene
41. St. John Chrysostom

Holy Popes
42. St. Pius V
43. St. Gregory
44. St. Leo

Holy Martyrs
45. St. Agnes
46. St. Cecilia
47. St. Maria Goretti

Holy Martyrs
48. St. Stephen
49. St. Blaise
50. St. Laurence

51. Lily of the Valley

B. The Inner Aisle Stained Glass Windows: Twin Windows

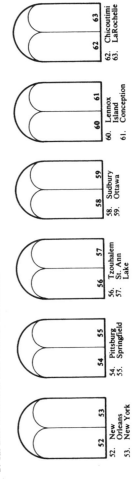

52. New Orleans
53. New York

54. Pittsburg
55. Springfield

56. Tzouhalem
57. St. Ann Lake

58. Sudbury
59. Ottawa

60. Lennox Island
61. Conception

62. Chicoutimi
63. LaRochelle

and the technique for their execution can best be illustrated by Auguste Labouret himself and Louis-N. Audet, architect of the Basilica:

"Saint Ann's stained glass windows are of the a new kind in America, for very few glass-painters have succeeded in mastering this art. The glass used in these windows must be perfectly clear and luminous in pieces one-inch thick and set, not in lead, but in reinforced concrete. The edges are chipped away with a hammer. Chipped in this manner, the glass pieces present numerous glittering facets ever twinkling in the sun. I dare say that these stained glass windows are the best ever produced since the Middle Ages. They are the work of Mr. Auguste Labouret, who invented this new technique ... In the spring of 1949, the United States glass-painters held a convention in Quebec.

Some of them had discovered these stained glass windows by chance and had hurried to fetch their trade-mates, who marvelled at such a richness of tone, produced by a technique totally unknown to them." (Louis-N. Audet, ASA, B-10a, b.14/doc. 17 781, p. 13-14).

"The window of chipped glass set in concrete has proved to be sturdy and nothing will prevent this translucent panel from being prefered to the flimsy lead-set one, because it will last as long as the building itself. It has lasting quality, it is waterproof, it is sturdy, it insulates from cold and heat, in a word, it is a reliable glass panel which requires no steel braces of any kind. The panel is firmly encased in a stone frame. The cement that cases the glass pieces is reinforced with steel mesh. A square foot of this type of glass pane weighs five times as much as a square foot of lead-set glass. (Auguste Labouret, ASA, B-10a, b.6/doc. 14 920).

"The Basilica is a house of prayer... The light that bathes the worshippers must harmonize with the interior decoration... The secret of atmosphere in Gothic cathedrals is light properly diffused. In this way, the church avoids tiring the eyes of the worshipper and helps him find his own interior light by isolating him from exterior things. To make a mistake of taste or consonance in the whole or part of this atmosphere is breaking the law of universal harmony" (Auguste Labouret, ABSA, 1943, p. 31).

The diagram herewith will help you identify each of the subjects represented in the stained glass windows.

1. The Bull's-Eyes of the Clerestory:

There are four bull's eyes, one at each corner of the nave. These windows present the *symbols of Christ* in the New Testament: the fountain of life, the Mystical Lamb, the crown of thorns with the nails, and the lily of the valley.

2. The Clerestory Triplets:

These large windows numbering thirty, but divided in triplets, illustrate the *litanies of the saints*. They portray the holy men and holy women of the Catholic Church, grouped in categories easily identifiable:

North side:

1. The holy Doctors of the Church (windows, 2, 3, 4): Saints: Francis of Sales, Thomas, Bonaventure.

2. The holy founders of religious orders (windows 5, 6, 7): Saints: Ignatius, Dominic, Vincent de Paul.

3. The holy priests: Saints: John Bosco (8), John Eudes (9), Philip Neri (10).

4. The holy laymen, Saints: Louis (11), Christopher (12), Isidore (13).

5. The holy women, Saints: Theresa of Avila (14), Frances Cabrini (15), Catherine of Sienna (16).

South side:

6. The Fathers of the Latin Church, Saints: Augustine (36), Jerome (37), Ambrose (38).

7. The Fathers of the Greek Church, Saints: Basil (39), John Damascene (40), John Chrysostom (41),.

8. The holy Popes, Saints: Pius V (42), Gregory (43), Leo (44).

9. The holy Martyrs, Saints: Agnes (45), Cecilia (46), Maria Goretti (47).

10. The holy Martyrs, Saints: Stephen (48), Blaise (49), Laurence (50).

This pictorial program illustrating the litanies of the saints is complete and ends with the stained glass windows in the nave.

3. The Twin Windows of the Inner Aisles:

The stained glass windows of the inner aisles belong to a pictorial program that begins to unfurl on the walls of the north transept and extends to the south transept; then, the program is continued in the nave. This program depicts the *spreading of the devotion of Saint Ann in America.* It begins with the first manifestation of devotion to Saint Ann before the foundation of the Sainte-Anne-de-Beaupré parish and it proceeds, over the years, to the present time. As the population of Quebec or Canada kept expanding, the people brought "their own Saint Ann" with them to their new settlements. The eager steadiness of the devotion's expansion shows in the dates inscribed on the windows. Each stained glass window memorializes a place where the devotion to Saint Ann kept growing over the years. In this system of 42 stained glass windows, the theme is developed as follows:

1. Growth of the devotion to Saint Ann at the time the country belonged to France: 18 windows in the transept.

2. Expansion of the same devotion throughout Quebec, after the British conquest: 6 windows in the nave.

3. The devotion to Saint Ann in the Canadian Provinces: 10 windows in the nave.

4. The devotion to Saint Ann in the United States: 8 windows at the back of the nave.

Each of these stained glass tableaux is made up of three elements:

1. A human figure, real or symbolic, representative of the place to be pictured.

2. At the bottom of the panel, the church or a typical element of the said place.

3. A decorative band bearing symbols of the same place.

For the visitor's convenience and to follow the present order of visit, the description of the stained glass windows is given here in the *reverse order* of the pictorial program. A more leisurely visit may be made later by following the dates marked on the windows.

Here is a sketchy presentation of the 24 stained glass windows of the nave with their main decorative elements:

North Side:

	Human Figure	Place	Symbolic Band
18. **New Haven,** Connecticut	**An Italian woman,** symbolizing Italian pilgrims	Saint Louis' church, Italian center of devotion to Saint Ann	**A rose,** Italy's national flower
19. **Trenton,** New Jersey	**Byzantine priest** At Trenton, there is a Byzantine center of devotion to Saint Ann	The Byzantine church at Trenton	**A Greek cross**
20. **Chicago,** Illinois	**A slaughter-house worker**	Saints Joachim and Ann's church, center of devotion to Saint Ann	**A shamrock** leaf (Irish clover) representing O'Brady's important group
21. **Detroit,** Michigan	**A Polish woman** pilgrim, dressed in her National clothes	Saint Ann's church	**A star,** indicating the beginning of the windows dedicated to the American centers
22. **Annaheim,** Saskat-chewan	**Neo-Canadians of the West.** A German man playing the flute	The church of Saint Ann of Annaheim, district of Muenster Abbey	**A wheat sheaf,** as seen on Saskatchewan's coat of arms
23. **Sainte-Anne-des-Chênes,** Manitoba	**A Red River pioneer.** The first settlers homesteaded near the oak forest when the east-west highway was being built	The church of Sainte-Anne-des-Chênes, served by the Redem-torist Fathers	**A bell;** the bells of Sainte-Anne-des-Chênes have "the most beau-tiful voices in the West".

24. **The Grove,** New Brunswick (near) Caraquet)	**A lobster fisherman.** Lobster-fishing is North New Brunswick's typical fishery	The Grove's church, near Caraquet	**A spread sail;** a similar one appears on New Brunswick's coat of arms
25. **Sainte-Anne-du-Ruisse,** near Yarmouth, Nova Scotia	**An Acadian woman.** Formerly, this Acadian parish was the meeting point of the Great Return	The church of Sainte-Anne-du-Ruisse (au)	**A star:** there is one on the Acadian flag and it symbolizes the Virgin
26. **Roquemaure,** (1934) Abitibi, Quebec	**An Abitibi lumberjack.** Logging was an important factor in the region's development	The former church of Sainte-Anne-de-Roquemaure, which was destroyed by fire	**A diamond;** like those used on diamond drills. Gold mines are foremost in the region
27. **Pointe-au-Père,** Rimouski, Quebec (1874)	**A ship captain** on the St. Lawrence River. The statue of the small shrine was given by ship captains of the St. Lawrence	The lighthouse of Pointe-au-Père	**An anchor;** symbolizing ship captains
28. **Montreal** (1841)	**Bishop Ignace Bourget.** Deeply devoted to Saint Ann, he revived the old shrine of Pointe-Saint-Charles	**The former** Redemptorist church of Saint Ann	**A Latin cross:** There is one on the Redemptorists' coat of arms and on Mont-Royal
29. **Beauce** (1778) Saint Mary's chapel	**Cardinal Taschereau.** The chapel was a fief of the Taschereau family	Saint Ann's chapel	**A maple leaf:** Beauce is maple leaf country

South Side:

52. **New Orleans,** Louisiana	**A black man** of the south; this Black man represents the	**Saint Ann's Grotto and Calvary;** a pilgrimage place	**A cotton flower;** Cotton growing is typical of the South

	numerous Black people who come to Sainte-Anne	in New Orleans	
53. **New York**	**Father Giasson** of the Order of the Holy Sacrament, an ardent promoter of the devotion to Saint Ann	Saint John the Baptist's church in New York, where miracles were worked when the Great Relic passed	**The globe;** New York is the seat of the United Nations
54. **Pittsburgh, Pennsylvania**	**Father James Cox,** one of the most ardent promoters of the devotion to Saint Ann	Pittsburgh's Cathedral	**A triangle;** Pittsburgh is the center of the coal industry, symbolized by a cross-ruled triangle as appears on Economy charts
55. **Springfield, Massachusetts**	**Andrew Ahearn's pilgrimage** of the sick	Springfield's Cathedral	**A fleur-de-lys;** Springfield is in the center of New England, where so many French-speaking Americans live
56. **Tzouhalem, British Columbia**	**Bishop Modeste Demers,** first Bishop of Victoria, an ardent promoter of the devotion to Saint Ann	"Butter Church", first chapel dedicated to Saint Ann on Victoria Island and paid by profits on the sale of butter by Father Rondeau	**The rising Sun;** it is pictured of the Province's coat of arms
57. **Lake Saint Ann,** Alberta	**A Prairie Indian.** National Shrine at St. Anne Lake	Lake Saint Ann's chapel	**A petroleum flame;** Alberta is black gold country
58. **Sudbury** Ontario	**An underground Miner;** Sudbury is nickel mining center	Saint Ann's church	**A diamond;** diamonds are used at the tip of a miner's drill

59. **Ottawa**	**Bishop Bruno Guigues O.M.I.** He consecrated his diocese, the Oblates and the Grey Sisters to Saint Ann	Saint Ann's church in Ottawa	**A silver heart;** Bishop Guigues had the Oblates and the Grey Sisters' names inscribed within a votive heart offered to Saint Ann
60. **Lennox Island,** Prince Edward Island	**An Oysterman,** at Malpèque Bay	The Indian chapel of Lennox Island's mission	**A rose;** Prince Edward Island is called "the Garden of the Atlantic"
61. **Conception,** Newfoundland	**A newfoundland Fisherman,** offering his fish nets	St. Ann-of-the-Conception's church, in the diocese of Havre-de-Grâce	**The rising sun:** Canada's first eastern province
62. **Chicoutimi** 1859	**A Saguenay Logroller.** Lumbering triggered the region's development	**Saint Ann's cross,** erected by Bishop Baillargeon to help prevent shipwrecks in Saguenay crossings	**Blueberries;** the blue manna of the rocks is the region's typical fruit
63. **LaRochelle,** 1857	**An Eastern-Townships Miner.** At LaRochelle, there is a granite mine. The Eastern Townships is asbestos country	Saint Ann's church in LaRochelle, formerly called "Stukely".	**A beech-nut cup;** The Eastern Townships is hard wood country

5. THE PEWS IN THE BASILICA:

For a more extensive study of the pews of the Basilica, the following book ought to be read, especially pages 15 to 39: *"The Pews in the Basilica of Sainte-Anne-de-Beaupré"*, by Father Laurent Proulx, C.Ss.R.

There are 260 pews in the nave of the Basilica, namely 80 twelve-foot pews, 52 nine-foot pews and 28 four-foot pews. They can seat 1 400 people in all. A greater seating capacity could have been provided, but the interior space of the Basilica was so arranged as to allow easy movement to the crowds during Eucharistic celebrations and, above all, processions. The pews were made by Nilus Leclerc Woodwork Inc. of L'Isletville.

The ornamental decoration of the pews was executed by a young Tyrol artist, *Franz Moroder,* an expert in wood carving.

The decorative program of the pews unfurls on the wide red oak endpanels. This ornamental program is double. One element which remains the same on each end of every pew is the scallop shell. It is the traditional symbol of pilgrims who used to carry such a shell as a drinking cup in their traveling-bag.

The other decorative element varies from one pew to another and appears only once in the whole system. An *animal* and a *plant* are carved on each pew. These are not symbols, but, as explains Father Proulx in the above mentioned book, "They were summoned there *for themselves"*. The idea was to gather all the creatures of the Universe and, as it were, have them join in the solemn hymn of praise offered here to the Lord. An effort was made to include animals and plants from all parts of the world, notwithstanding a choice place for those of Canada and the United States. For a detailed visit of this fauna and flora, Father Laurent Proulx's book is helpful. Here is just an example of the work as seen on the last five pews at the back of the nave:

South Side		North Side	
Animals	**Plants**	**Animals**	**Plants**
Royal eagle	Wild rose	Buffalo	Spikenard
Prairie dog	Mayflower	Porcupine	Laciniate rudbekia
Ground turtle	Thorn-apple	Bee	Foxgloves
Grizzly bear	Cotoneaster	Black bear	Cluster cherries
Woodpecker	Montmorency Cherry	Great horned Owl	Raspberries

6. The floor of the nave:

1. Concrete Casting of the Floor:

Before 1934, the present floor which makes up the vault of the crypt did not exist. After the temporary chapel had been destroyed by fire, the space of the nave was fitted up for immediate use. The floor of this "temporary church" was that of the crypt and its roof was a temporary structure reaching to the vaults of the outer aisles, where the existing confessionals are. More details on the dimensions of this temporary church are given on page 20 of the book: *"Sainte-Anne-de-Beaupré, Past and Present Churches"*, by G.U. Gagnon, C.Ss.R. In 1934, it was decided to cast the floor of the Basilica, but, in so doing, *another church* had to be cast, namely the present crypt with its pillars and arches. Months and months of work were required to set in place the wooden forms that would arch the crypt vault over cross-shaped pillars as we see it today. A total of 235 000 feet of wood was needed for the forms. About mid-January 1934, the concrete casting was begun and went on until 5 176 tons of concrete were poured in; an aggregate of 612 tons of cement, 2 645 tons of crushed stone, 1 490 tons of sand and 154 tons of iron rods. The metal framework looked quite complicated with its steel pillars branching out into crisscrossed iron rods, tied at every six-inch length and arched in four directions. The concrete casting went from the ambulatory on to the nave through the sanctuary and the transept. When the concrete had sufficiently set, the floor was entirely covered with terrazzo. Such was the floor of the Basilica for 25 years.

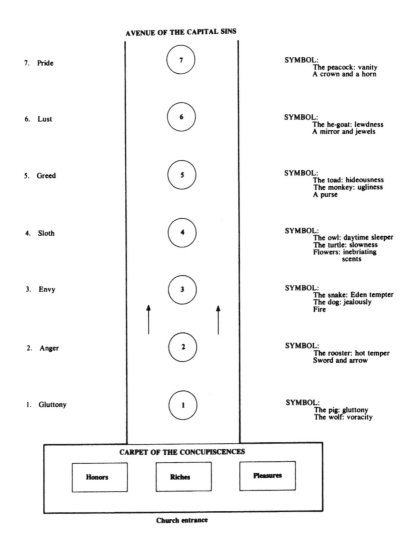

AVENUE OF THE CAPITAL SINS

7. Pride

7

SYMBOL:
The peacock: vanity
A crown and a horn

6. Lust

6

SYMBOL:
The he-goat: lewdness
A mirror and jewels

5. Greed

5

SYMBOL:
The toad: hideousness
The monkey: ugliness
A purse

4. Sloth

4

SYMBOL:
The owl: daytime sleeper
The turtle: slowness
Flowers: inebriating
    scents

3. Envy

3

SYMBOL:
The snake: Eden tempter
The dog: jealously
Fire

2. Anger

2

SYMBOL:
The rooster: hot temper
Sword and arrow

1. Gluttony

1

SYMBOL:
The pig: gluttony
The wolf: voracity

CARPET OF THE CONCUPISCENCES

| Honors | Riches | Pleasures |

Church entrance

2. The Pavement of the Basilica:

In 1958, at last, the floor received its long-awaited pavement. The floor of the ambulatory and the sanctuary had already been paved. That year, the pavement of the transept and of the nave was undertaken.

The *central passageway* of the nave, that of the *aisles* and the surface of the *transept* were to be paved with ceramic mosaic. The remaining surface, namely underneath the pews and in all the other passages, were to be covered with gray-toned *tiles:* "fur grey" under the pews and "shore pebble" in secondary passages.

This decoration project was entirely committed to a mosaic expert, who had already worked on the central vault and on the radiating chapels: *Walter del Mistro,* whose name is identified with all the mosaic work executed at Saint Ann's Shrine.

The two decorative systems to be observed in the nave are the *entrance carpet* depicting the three concupiscences and the *central passage* or avenue picturing the *capital sins.* The details on these decorations are given on pages 7 to 15 in a book by Father Laurent Proulx, C.Ss.R. *"The Mosaic Pavements of Saint Ann's Basilica".* The book ought to be read for a thorough visit of the church. The diagram herewith merely shows the chosen subjects with their symbols.

7. The Wall under the Choir Loft:

(Before leaving your point of observation, you are invited to turn around and take time to observe the admirable decoration on the wall below the choir loft).

A. The Tympanums:

There are 5 sculptured tympanums above the doors of the Basilica; the carving was done again by two artists who produced the capitals, the corner sculptures and the stations of the cross: Émile Brunet who submitted the clay models and Maurice Lord, who carved them out of Indiana stone. The subject chosen for the three *major tympanums* was Jesus' *pilgrimages* during his life on earth.

THE DECORATION OF THE WALL BELOW THE CHOIR LOFT

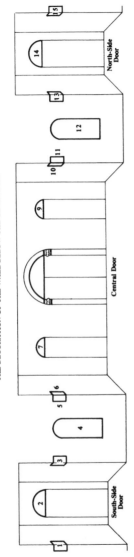

1. The Hidden Treasure: capital carved by J. Pagé
2. Jesus' Entry into Jerusalem: Tympanum carved by Brunet and Lord
3. The Coveted Pearl: Capital carved by J. Pagé
4. Niche and Statue of Saint Anthony of Padua: niche background in mosaic with lily-patterned border by Walter del Mistro
   White marble statue by sculptor DeRosa
5. Probable portrait of Paul-O. Parent, foreman for the stone-cutting work of Deschambault Co., made at the Company's
   factory by the Company's sculptors
6. Portrait of Louis-N. Audet, architect of the Basilica by the same sculptors
7. Small tympanum: a boat in full sail: Brunet and Lord
8. Big tympanum of the central door: Jesus visiting the Temple: Brunet and Lord
9. Small tympanum: birds drinking from a cup: Brunet and Lord
10. Mr. Coulombe, assistant of his foreman nephew, Jean Coulombe
11. Mr. Jean Coulombe, foreman for Collet & Frères Co., which finished the interior of the Basilica.
    Work by the sculptors of Deschambault Co.
12. Niche and statue of Saint Theresa of the Infant Jesus: mosaic background with rose-patterned border by Walter del Mistro.
    Statue by DeRosa, Chiesa Nuova.
13. A fishnet: capital carved by J. Pagé
14. Tympanum above the north-side door: The Disciples of Emmaus on the road. Brunet and Lord
15. The Mustard Seed: capital carved by Jean Pagé

65

1. The Tympanum above the central Door: "At twelve years of age, Jesus visits the Temple with his parents" (8 on the diagram)
2. The Tympanum above the North-Side Door: "Jesus walks with the disciples of Emmaus" (14 on the diagram)
3. The Tympanum above the South-Side Door: "Christ destined to die during his last pilgrimage" (2 on the diagram)
4. The Tympanum above the small Door between the central and the north-side Doors: Two birds drinking from the cup of life (9 on the diagram)
5. The Tympanum on the small Door, between the central Door and the south-side Door: A boat in full sail with Christ's monogram (7 on the diagram)

B. The Capitals of the Parables:

Four capitals, flanking the side-doors, were assigned to the pictorial representation of the parables. They were carved at the same time as the capital of the aisles, where is pictured the story of salvation from Adam to Jesus. The four capitals were carved by Jean Pagé of the "École des Beaux Arts", Quebec.

1. The mustard seed (15 on the diagram) North side.
2. A fish net (13 on the diagram) North side.
3. The coveted pearl (3 on the diagram) South side.
4. The hidden treasure (1 on the diagram) South side.

C. The Memorial Capitals of the Main Entrance:

The finish work of the Basilica was done by Collet & Frères Co. of Montreal. The company's foreman was Jean Coulombe, whose assistant and uncle was Joseph Coulombe. The stone was supplied by a Montreal firm, Deschambault Company, directed by master stone-cutter Paul O. Parent. At the completion of the finish work, which lasted many seasons, if we include the finish of the sanctuary, the transept and especially the nave, the workers wanted to immortalize in stone the memory of those responsible for this great work. Hence, the four figures seen in the decorative band running all along the arcades. These sculptures are in the *recess near the central door* and were executed by stone-cutters of Deschambault Co. Nothing more is known about those sculptors.

North Side
1. Jean Coulombe, foreman for Collet & Frère, Co. (11 on the diagram)
2. Joseph Coulombe, assistant foreman for Collet & Frères, Co. (10)

South Side
3. Louis-N. Audet, architect of the Basilica (6)
4. Paul-O. Parent, master stone-cutter for Deschambault Co. (5)

D. The Niches and Statues:

Finally, two niches were provided at the back of the Basilica to honor two popular saints, who didn't have their altar around the sanctuary: Saint Anthony of Padua (4 on the diagram) and Saint Theresa of the Infant Jesus (12 on the diagram). Saint Theresa's niche on the north side and Saint Anthony's on the south side, are similar. They are framed by an arch and contain a white marble statue carved by De Rosa at Chiesa Nuova, Italy. The base of the statue is of black granite quarried at Alma. It is the material that was used for the base of the pillars, the columns and all the other decorated parts of the Basilica. The statues stand against a mosaic background executed by Walter del Mistro; this background decoration shows a border of roses for Saint Theresa and a border of lilies for Saint Anthony.

5. VISIT OF THE AISLES

(For the visit of the aisles, we suggest that you follow the direction indicated on the diagram. There will be a first stop on the south side, at the back of the inner aisle and a second one at about the front of the outer aisle. This side has been chosen because it is usually less crowded than the north side where more people pass on their way to the great statue and the Relic altar).

1. The Inner Aisles:

The *inner aisles* are 18 feet, or 5,4 metres, wide and 45 feet or 13,7 metres, high; like the nave they open out on the transept.

SUGGESTED DIRECTION FOR THE VISIT

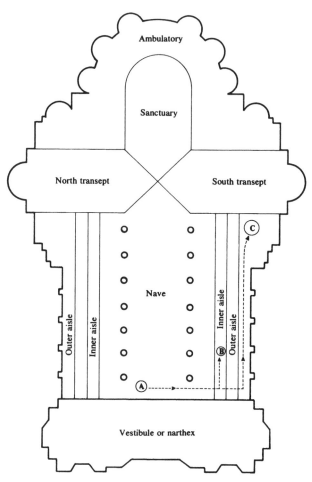

A. Place where you were for the explanations of the nave

B. Stop, at the entrance of the south inner aisle

C. Stop for the explanations of the south outer aisle

Contrary to the nave, the aisles are not barrel-vaulted, but their ceiling is a series of small vaults, namely six *groined vaults* and two *hanging cupolas*. The inner aisles are bordered on one side by the pillars of the outer aisle. The highlights of these inner aisles are: *the decoration of the vaults* and the *stations of the cross.*

a. The Vaults of the Inner Aisles:

Many years had elapsed since the casting of these vaults when it was decided to give them their final decoration. This work was assigned to Walter del Mistro in January 1966. The details of the pictorial project for the vaults and cupolas are given on pages 22 to 38 of the book of Father Laurent Proulx, C.Ss.R., *"The Secondary Vaults in Saint-Anne's Basilica".* You will find here only a few words on the subject. The decoration of the vaults was inspired by Psalm 94 which is a psalm of travel or pilgrimage. It is a prayer written for a procession and this kind of celebration takes place daily at Saint Ann's Shrine. When a procession cannot by held outdoors on account of bad weather, the crowds walk indoors in procession through the church, singing hymns and reciting prayers. We will mention only five verses as they appear at the entrance of the inner aisles from the stopping point suggested for the visit. For more information, please refer to Father Proulx's book.

The pictorial program, inspired by the psalm, begins to unfurl from the side of the north transept; it runs all along the inner aisle from front to back; then, it skips to the other side near the point where you are standing, to continue along the south side from back to front. Thus, the verses you can see now are from the second half of the psalm, but each verse has its own symbolical value:

"For He is our God". The triangle framing the name of the "one God" in three persons, is the traditional symbol of the Trinity.

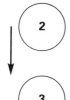

"We, the People whose Shepherd He is". The Lord is pictured as a shepherd: the Good Shepherd.

"The Flock led by his Hand". Three lambs represent the flock protected by God's blessing.

"If you only listened to my Voice today". A prophet proclaims the good news of salvation, but three passersby do not pay attention.

"Don't close your Heart as if in Strife". In the history of God's people, these were difficult times when decisions were taken against the will of God. The people with a "stiff neck", symbolizing resistance to God, namely our sins, is portrayed here by a haughty figure in the medallion.

b. The Stations of the Cross inside the Basilica:

In the lower part of each column of the nave, was placed a station of the way of the cross in relief. Here again Émile Brunet submitted the clay models and Maurice Lord translated them into Indiana stone. The decision to have these stations was taken on November 28, 1954 and, in the following months, the stations were installed one by one as soon as they were ready. Émile Brunet himself explains the idea that inspired his work:

"I finally managed to produce truly impressive compositions, expressing the various tragic phases of Our Lord's sufferings and the compassion of the holy women, of Veronica and of Saint John, while eliminating all unnecessary figures." (ASA, B-10, b.2/doc. 19,341)

"Paramount among our preoccupations was that of giving preeminence to Christ's figure. He must always be in the forefront". (ASA, B-10, b.2/doc. 19 358)

All this has produced discreet yet very impressive bas-reliefs, the face of Christ being the most striking. The artist has created an exquisite harmony of lines especially in the drapery of the robes and the masterful position of the body and the limbs. Saint Ann's Shrine needed this prolonged meditation on the mystery of human suffering, which draws its real value from participation to the passion of Christ.

2. The Outer Aisles:

(For this explanation, we suggest going to point C of the diagram, where there is more light and from where an overall perspective view of the south outer aisle is possible).

The outer aisle is the part of the church which, according to plan, receives the least amount of light. This was necessary to provide a zone of discretion and reflexion around the confessionals lining the aisle. Here are some points of interest which we would like to explain:

1. The Decoration of the Vaults:

Similar to that of the inner aisles, the ceiling of the outer aisles is made up of groined vaults, but these are smaller than the former. Here, a simple ornamental decoration was deemed sufficient: sparse lines around the lights and a few arabesques on the upper corner of the pillars and pilasters. This work was done also by Walter del Mistro.

2. The Capitals of the Outer Aisles:

The decoration for the capitals of the outer aisles was inspired by an old decorative theme used in the Middle Ages: the *"tree of Jesse"*. Jesse was king David's father and Jesus, the Messiah, was born from David's royal lineage. In the Middles Ages, decorators often used a motif similar to a family genealogical tree. They represented a tree whose trunk personified Jesse, the father of David, and ramified branches which stood for the descendants of royal lineage all the way up to

Jesus. This theme was further extended in the decoration of the capitals of the outer aisles. The idea was to make it, as it were, a history of salvation including Saint Ann and other outstanding personages in the messianic expectation. The pictorial project was entrusted to sculptor Louis Pagé of the "École des Beaux-Arts" of Quebec. He carved the 24 capitals with the help of some of his pupils in 1965.

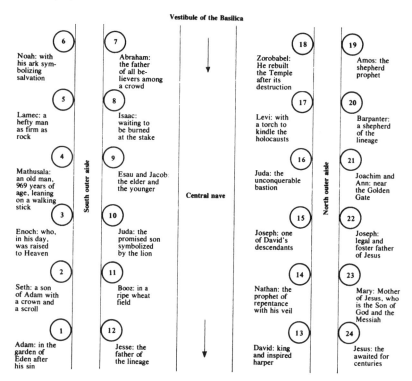

Vestibule of the Basilica

6 Noah: with his ark symbolizing salvation

7 Abraham: the father of all believers among a crowd

18 Zorobabel: He rebuilt the Temple after its destruction

19 Amos: the shepherd prophet

5 Lamec: a hefty man as firm as rock

8 Isaac: waiting to be burned at the stake

17 Levi: with a torch to kindle the holocausts

20 Barpanter: a shepherd of the lineage

4 Mathusala: an old man, 969 years of age, leaning on a walking stick

9 Esau and Jacob: the elder and the younger

South outer aisle

Central nave

North outer aisle

16 Juda: the unconquerable bastion

21 Joachim and Ann: near the Golden Gate

3 Enoch: who, in his day, was raised to Heaven

10 Juda: the promised son symbolized by the lion

15 Joseph: one of David's descendants

22 Joseph: legal and foster father of Jesus

2 Seth: a son of Adam with a crown and a scroll

11 Booz: in a ripe wheat field

14 Nathan: the prophet of repentance with his veil

23 Mary: Mother of Jesus, who is the Son of God and the Messiah

1 Adam: in the garden of Eden after his sin

12 Jesse: the father of the lineage

13 David: king and inspired harper

24 Jesus: the awaited for centuries

3. The Small Stained Glass Windows of the Outer Aisles:

Like those of the nave, they were made of thick chipped glass set in concrete by Auguste Labouret of Paris. These windows above the confessionals illustrate the *history* of the devotion to Saint Anne here at Sainte-Anne-de-Beaupré. All the people who are known to have efficiently promoted this devotion, people who have influenced the history of veneration for the saint at Sainte-Anne-de-Beaupré are pictured here in *ten stained glass windows.*

South-side outer aisle	Small stained glass windows	North-side outer aisle
1898 (10	Father Victor Charland, a Dominican who wrote the detailed history of the devotion to Saint Ann throughout the world and especially in America	Frederic de Ghyvelde. A Franciscan better known by the name of "Good Father Frederic" who wrote a popular biography of Saint Ann **9**) 1896
1879 (8	Fathers Girard, Tielen, Lamontagne and Clement Leclerc, Redemptorists who worked so much on behalf of Saint Ann at the turn of the century	Father N.-A. Leclerc, founder of the Annals of St.-Anne de Beaupré. A book and a pen and double-toned maple leaves symbolizing publication in two languages **7**) 1873
1696 (6	Pierre Lemoyne d'Iber-ville. In the middle of a heroic situation, he made a vow to Saint Ann. The Shrine has a crucifix that belonged to him	Sir Prouville de Tracy, one of Saint Ann's great devotees, who donated an ex-voto signaling a miracle **5**) 1666
1664? (4	Fr. Thomas Morel, first parish priest of Sainte-Anne and of the domain of Beaupré. The chapel is that of 1658	Étienne de Lessard: he donated the land occupied by the Shrine. Freshly plowed furrows and wheat stalks **3**) 1658
1658 (2	Gabriel Thubières de Queylus, a Sulpician, then parish priest of Quebec, who named the parish for Saint Ann. The Sulpicians' coat of arms	Father Joseph Poncet, a Jesuit, who founded the Confraternity of Saint Ann in 1657. The coat of arms is that of the Society of Jesus. The palm leaf represents the hardships suffered for the faith by Father Poncet **1**)

4. The Confessionals:

In the outer aisles of the Basilica, there are 24 confessionals produced by the Deslauriers workshop in Montreal. They are placed in pairs and are made up of three partitions, the center one having a higher pinnacle. Inside the Basilica, the confessionals present the gable-shaped ornamental motif that is also displayed above the doors outside the church. The thick, glassed doors of the confessionals close automatically; when the penitent kneels down, a red pilot light goes on outside signaling his presence. The confessionals are made of white oak, quartersawed to show the beautiful watery pattern of the wood grain, enhanced by clear flat varnish. They were installed in the Basilica in 1958. In the back of the church, there are two confessionals with wider doors for the convenience of people in wheel-chairs.

6. THE TRANSEPT

(You are invited now to proceed to the center of the transept crossing, near the spot where the pavement bears an ornamental symbol of the tree of Eden. From there an overall view of the transept will be possible).

"The transept is of the same height and width as the nave. Its aisles are extensions of the inner aisles of the church and have the same proportions. At both ends, there are three vast windows, 40 feet high, and enclosed within a great arch with voussoirs and columns. Under each of these windows, there is an apsidal chapel". (Father J.T. Nadeau, ABSA, 1923, p. 205)

When the finish work on the transept was begun in 1950, some alterations were made, so as to allow two altars to be placed on the sides of each chapel at the end of the transept.

Moreover, the engineers estimated that the end wall of the transept, pierced at the bottom with the large chapel openings, could not safely support the tremendous weight of the stone

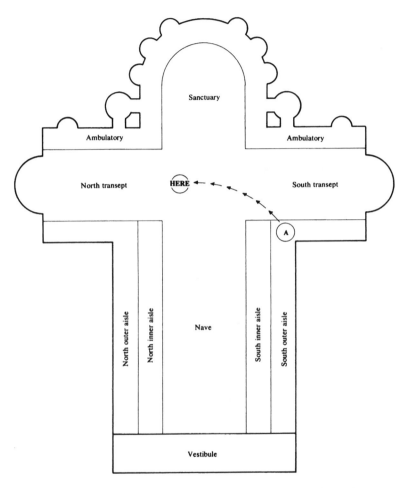

Sanctuary

Ambulatory

Ambulatory

North transept

HERE

South transept

A

North outer aisle

North inner aisle

South inner aisle

South outer aisle

Nave

Vestibule

coating. Consequently, the openings of the chapels were framed with a sturdy steel structure whose two pillars went all the way, through the floor, down to the rock below the church. The two steel pillars, weighing a total of 19 tons, support a wall of Texas Travertine (Cordova stone) with sculptured parts of Indiana stone.

A. THE VAULT MOSAICS OF THE TRANSEPT

The mosaic here follows the same technique as that of the nave described before and was executed by the same artists: Jean Gaudin and Auguste Labouret. The overall vault decoration of the transept is a part of the same pictorial program developed on the central vault, namely *Saint Ann's life on earth*. The transept crossing graphically represents the virtues of Saint

THE MOSAICS OF THE TRANSEPT

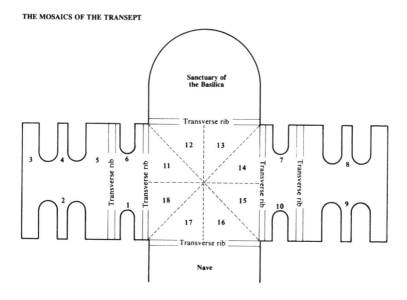

1. Saint Ann's wedding
2. Saint Ann and Saint Joachim performing acts of charity
3. Saint Ann deploring her sterility
4. Saint Joachim chased to the desert
5. Saint Joachim in the desert
6. News of the impending birth of the Blessed Virgin
7. Meeting near the Golden Gate
8. The daily chores of Saint Ann
9. Birth of the Virgin
10. Education of the Virgin

11. Justice
12. Prudence
13. Temperance (Cardinal virtues of Saint Ann)
14. Fortitude
15. Work
16. Mortification
17. Meekness (Familial virtues of Saint Ann)
18. Prayer

Ann. The motif is a seated symbolic figure holding up a shield with the picture of an animal or an object that symbolizes a virtue. All this is well explained in Father Proulx's book: *"The Central Arch in the Basilica of Sainte-Anne-de-Beaupré"*, pages 64 and 65.

1. Saint Ann's *cardinal* virtues:
   a. Justice, symbolized by the balance
   b. Prudence, symbolized by the snake
   c. Temperance, symbolized by the camel
   d. Fortitude, symbolized by the lion

2. *Familial* virtues of Saint Ann:
   a. Work, symbolized by the ox
   b. Mortification, symbolized by a myrrh plant
   c. Meekness, symbolized by the lamb
   d. Prayer, symbolized by a censer

B. THE STAINED GLASS WINDOWS OF THE TRANSEPT:

The transept is lighted by forty thick stained glass windows executed by Auguste Larouret's workshop, according to the process explained before in this book. There are five different pictorial programs developed in the windows of the transept:

1. The Great stained Glass Windows at the Ends of the Transept:

At either end of the transept, there is a set of three tall windows, 41/4 feet wide, separated by walls bearing decorative columns. Those giant triplets are meant to memorialize two great shrines where Saint Ann is honored as well as in Beaupré: Saint Ann of *Jerusalem* and Saint Ann of *Auray,* Brittany, France. It is customary for a stained glass panel to contain one human figure together with a few symbols. Here, the glass-painter, having a very vast surface to cover, added to each human figure a typical scene relating, so to speak, the history of each shrine, in the manner of historiated stained glass windows of the Middle Ages. The two giant triplets of the transept were installed in 1949.

Saint Ann of Jerusalem: South End of the Transept:

In Jerusalem, near the so-called Probation Pool, according to an old tradition, Saint Ann's house, where the Virgin was born, has constantly been revered. Not long after the Council of Ephesus around 431, a church dedicated to Saint Ann stood there. And there has always been a church at that place. The existing church was built in the XIIth century. Saint Ann of Jerusalem was entrusted to the White Fathers in 1878, the very year the Redemptorists were given control over the Basilica of Sainte-Anne-de-Beaupré. Since 1934, *Saint Ann of Jerusalem* is a minor Basilica like Sainte-Anne-de-Beaupré. The stained glass window memorializes, not only Saint Ann of Jerusalem, but its extension into the Provence tradition, going as far as in Provence, France. At *Sainte-Anne d'Apt,* in Provence, are kept famous relics of Saint Ann, of which many have been sent to various places throughout the world. Provence is the place where some friends of Jesus lived, namely Saint *Mary Magdalen* celebrated on the feast of Sainte-Beaume, and *Lazarus,* first Bishop of Marseille.

The window depicting Saint Ann of Jerusalem shows Saint Ann as she is venerated in Jerusalem. On her right, stands Saint Lazarus as a Bishop with, over his head, a medallion picturing the Annunciation to the Virgin; on Saint Ann's left, appears Mary Magdalen under a medallion representing her at the foot of Jesus' cross. At the bottom of the window, above the inscription: "Good Saint Ann, protect our families", is pictured an immense crowd of people with a relic exposed for their veneration. This is to recall the arrival of Saint Ann's relic at Marseille. (ASA, B-10b, b.1/doc 20 014)

Saint Ann of Auray, Brittany: North end of the Transept:

A few years before the inauguration of Sainte-Anne-de-Beaupré, Saint Ann made an apparition in Brittany to a peasant named Nicolazic. Following his indications, an old statue of Saint Ann was found buried in a field at Bocenno. In 1625, with the permission of the Bishop of Vannes, pilgrimages to the first chapel began. Today, in the Basilica of Sainte-Anne-d'Auray is one of the great places of pilgrimage in France. In the window memorializing Sainte-Anne-d'Auray,

> "The saint of Auray is in the center with her daughter; at the bottom, a procession takes place in front of the Basilica at Auray with people dressed in their national clothes. The window, on the left, shows Nicolazic with the statue he has just found; above him, shipwrecked fishermen. The window on the right shows Keriolet, Auray's famous pilgrim with a traveling-bag and a walking-stick. The top part of this window continues the preceding scene: the fishermen go back to sea and have a plentiful draft. So, they gratefully offer their nets". (Eugène Lefebvre, C.Ss.R., ABSA, 1949, p. 198)

At the bottom of the window, the following inscription: "Good Saint Ann, protect France and Canada".

2. The Triplets in the Upper Part of the Transept:

The eight triplets in the upper part of the transept recall the Gospel theme of the *Beatitudes*. These windows were treated in a more decorative way than the windows of the nave. There is only one human figure in each panel and the text of the Beatitude covers the whole set of three panels in the window. The various subjects can be identified with the help of the diagram given in this book.

3. The Bull's-Eyes on the Transept:

There are four bull's-eyes at the height of the triplets of the Beatitudes and two more on the side of the sanctuary at the height of the twin windows of the nave.

1. The Bull's-Eyes at the Height of the Triplets:

Here, as in the nave, the windows represent *symbols of Christ,* namely:

The Star of David: window 75	One the west side of the transept
The Phoenix: window 76	On the nave side
Noah's Ark: window 147	On the side of the transept
The Ark of the Covenant: window 148	On the sanctuary side

A. Windows of the Clerestory: Triplets and Bull's-Eyes

69-71
"Blessed are
those who suffer
persecution for
justice"

| 69 | 70 | 71 |

72-74
"Blessed are
the peace-
makers"

| 72 | 73 | 74 |

75
Star of
David

76
The Phoenix

77-79
"Blessed are the
clean of heart"

| 77 | 78 | 79 |

80-82
"Blessed are
the merciful"

| 80 | 81 | 82 |

92-131

132-140

B. The Twin Windows of the Transept

161
Restigouche

83
Jeremy Islets
84
Yamachiche

| 83 | 84 |

85
La Pocatière
86
Bellevue

| 85 | 86 |

87
Verchères
88
Varennes

| 87 | 88 |

89
Lamothe Island
90
Quebec

| 89 | 90 |

162
Cape Breton

C. Staircase Windows

91
Saint Ann's
Aides

92
The Ladies of
Saint Ann

**D. Stained glass
windows in
the façade**

92-131
The Rose
Litanies to the Virgin
132-140
Decorative windows (9)

80

2. The Bull's-Eye at the Height of the Twin Windows:

This pictorial system continues the decoration of the *sanctuary* where the four Evangelists are pictured at the crossing of the transept and the sanctuary. Window num. 157 depicting Saint Mark and the one picturing Saint John decorate the corner of the sanctuary on the south side. Window num. 158 dedicated to Saint Matthew and the one picturing Saint Luke decorate the north-side corner of the sanctuary.

4. The Twin Windows of the Transept:

A. The Windows in the West Wall *Facing the Nave.*

These windows belong to the pictorial program developed in the nave and represent the local expansion of the devotion to Saint Ann in Canada and in the United States. More precisely, they memorialize the expansion of the devotion at the origin of the country, under the French Regime, when the country was called Nouvelle France. Two simple windows, beside the double windows in the transept near the ends, were included in this pictorial program. In the diagram they bear the numbers 161 and 162.

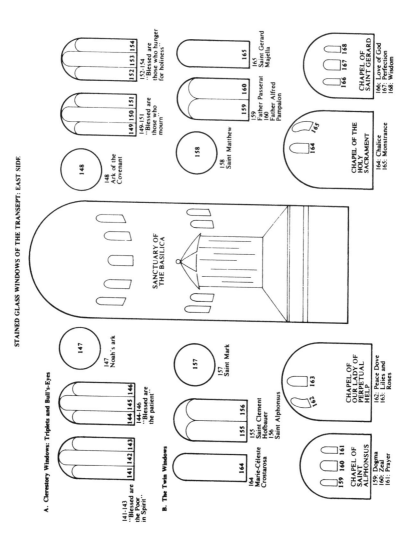

STAINED GLASS WINDOWS OF THE TRANSEPT: EAST SIDE

A. Clerestory Windows: Triplets and Bull's-Eyes

152 | 153 | 154
152-154
"Blessed are
those who hunger
for holiness"

149 | 150 | 151
149-151
"Blessed are
those who
mourn"

148
Ark of the
Covenant

147
Noah's ark

144 | 145 | 146
144-146
"Blessed are
the patient"

141 | 142 | 143
141-143
"Blessed are
the Poor
the Spirit"

165
Saint Gerard
Majella

166 | 167 | 168
CHAPEL OF
SAINT GERARD
166: Love of God
167: Perfection
168: Wisdom

159 | 160
159
Father Passerat
160
Father Alfred
Pampalon

164 | 165
CHAPEL OF THE
HOLY
SACRAMENT
164: Chalice
165: Monstrance

158
Saint Matthew

SANCTUARY OF
THE BASILICA

157
Saint Mark

B. The Twin Windows

155 | 156
155
Saint Clement
Hofbauer
156
Saint Alphonsus

164
Marie-Céleste
Crostarosa

162 | 163
CHAPEL OF
OUR LADY OF
PERPETUAL
HELP
162: Peace Dove
163: Lilies and
Roses

159 | 160 | 161
CHAPEL OF
SAINT
ALPHONSUS
159: Dogma
160: Zeal
161: Prayer

Human Figure	Place Symbol	Symbolic Band
Window 162: **Father Vimont,** **Cape Breton** Jesuit. At the time **1629** of Quebec's surrender to the British, he landed at Cape Breton with Captain Daniel; it was then the only French territory in Canada. It was under Saint Ann's protection.	A French ship	**A Fleur-de-lys,** France's floral emblem
Window 90: **Jean Levasseur,** **Québec** founder of the **1657** "Carpenter's Fraternity of Lady Saint Ann", in Saint Ann's chapel, Quebec.	The Levasseur family's coat of arms	**A stylized nail;** symbolizing carpentry
Window 89: **A Canadian Soldier.** **Lamothe** Carignan's regiment **Island** was sent to Fort **1666** Saint-Ann on Lamothe Island in Lake Champlain	Fort Saint Ann's chapel	**A star:** to recall that today this is American territory
Window 88: **A Canadian Farmer.** **Varennes** Varennes is a rural parish with an agricultural vocation	The miraculous image of Varennes, crowned by Bishop Bourget	**An ear of wheat**
Window 87: **Madeleine de Ver-** **Laperade** **chères,** a national **1693** heroin, married to Sir Tarieu de la Pérade.	The church of Laperade	**An arrowhead**
Window 86: **A Woodsman.** **Bellevue** After Saint Louis, **1710** Saint Ann became the patron saint of the parish, because woodsmen used to stop there to pray Saint Ann.	The church of Bellevue	**Flames,** symbolizing the legend of will-o'-the-wisps

Window 85: **La Pocatière** 1715	**Father Painchaud**	Sainte-Anne-de-la-Pocatière College	**A cross,** symbolizing the great Mission cross at La Pocatière
Windor 84: **Yamachiche** 1718	**"A woman designed by God",** from a poem by Nérée Beauchemin who praised the Canadian woman protected in her home by Saint Ann.	The church at Yamachiche. It is the former church, which was destroyed by fire	**Wedding rings**
Window 83: **Jeremy Islets** 1735	**A Trapper of the North,** who pictures Jeremy of the Mountain, an assiduous pilgrim to Sainte-Anne-de-Beaupré and one of the pioneers on the North Coast	The chapel at Jeremy Islets, meeting place of the Montagnais indian tribe in July	**A snow flake,** symbolizing the latitude of the region
Window 161: **Restigouche** 1740	**A Micmac Indian,** typical of the Restigouche reserve	The chapel among wigwams	**A trap** or stylized snare

B. The Twin Windows in the West Wall *around the Sanctuary:*

The pictorial program of the windows memorializes the great personages of the Redemptorist Order, whose members were entrusted with the parish and the pilgrimage organization at Sainte-Anne-de-Beaupré, about one century ago, namely in December 1878. This program is developed in six stained glass panels pertaining to the twin windows and the two simple windows, at the same height, at the ends of the transept.

Here are the personages memorialized in the stained glass windows:

Window 165: at the north end of the transept.

Venerable Marie-Céleste-Crostarosa, foundress of the Redemptoristines. This Order, which originated at the same time as the Redemptorist Order, has a convent at Sainte-Anne-de-Beaupré, adjoining Saint Gerard's church on the hill.

Window 155: **Saint Clement-Mary Hofbauer,** the apostle of Vienna and second founder of the Redemptorist Order: he was responsible for its development outside Italy.

Window 154: **Saint Alphonsus Liguori,** founder of the Redemptorist Order, Bishop of Santa Agatha and Doctor of the Church.

Window 159: **Saint Jean Neumann,** a Redemptorist of Czech origin, third Bishop of Philadelphia; canonized by Pope Paul VI in 1977.

Window 160: The servant of God, **Alfred Pampalon,** a Canadian Redemptorist who lived in the second half of the last century and whose cause for beatification is being introduced in the Roman Catholic Church. In the Chapel of the Immaculate Conception, one can pray beside the reliquary in which his remains are kept.

Window 165: **Saint Gerard Majella,** a Redemptorist Brother, a great miracle-worker and the special protector of expectant mothers. He is honored under this last title by the members of the "League of Saint Gerard".

5. The Small Stained Glass Windows:

There are four small windows in the lower part of the transept and two others near the stairway leading to the crypt.

1. In the two stained glass windows *below the simple windows* of the transept on the sanctuary side, there are two symbols referring to the church itself. They emphasize the role of the Basilica as "House of God" and "Door of Heaven", two invocations taken from the litanies to the Virgin.

2. The Two Small Stained Glass Windows *near the Stairways.*

Here, as in Hunter's sculptures at the entrance of the Basilica, are represented the two kinds of supernatural interventions observed at the shrine:

a. The invocation "Refugium peccatorum" or "Refuge for sinners", taken from the litanies to the Virgin, is illustrated by a radiating lily growing out of a heart encircled by a snake. This symbol represents conversion of the heart.

b. The other invocation "Salus infirmorum", or "Salvation for the infirm", is shown as the star of hope shining between crutches linked by thorns, and represents the cures performed at Saint-Anne's.

3. The Two Stained Glass Windows in the Stairway leading to the crypt.

a. The *"Ladies of Saint Ann":* north side

For a century, many associations of married women had adopted Saint Ann as their patroness and called themselves "Ladies of Saint Ann"; today they are called "Christian Women". Their stained glass window recalls their motto: "Be of help" and their fields of apostolate: the Church, the family and the parish. Three things are pictured here: the coat of arms of the Ladies of Saint Ann, their statute book and the little beads of Saint Ann.

b. *Saint Ann's Aides:* south side

During the 1948-1949 winter, a few young men formed an association in order to give assistance to the sick pilgrims at the Shrine. In recent years, they have also offered aid wherever needed and have especially helped organizing the processions. Saint Ann's Aides now belong to a Sodality numbering hundreds of active members. The stained glass window memorializing their presence at the Shrine, pictures their motto: "Faith, Charity, Self-Sacrifice" and their distinctive symbols: Saint Ann's Aides' coat of arms and a wheel-chair.

C. The Sculptures of the Transept: Capitals, corner works and column-statues

1. Capitals and Corner Works:

The decorative system of sculptures for the capitals and corner works of the vane is continued through the transept, but with the only difference that the corner works of the pillars, at the opening of the sanctuary, bear no pictorial symbols. The decoration of the latter is an ornamental pattern in the style of many other capitals and arches in the church. An attentive observer will notice that, for the capitals of the columns decorating the walls or those supporting arches, the ornamental motif varies from one capital to another,

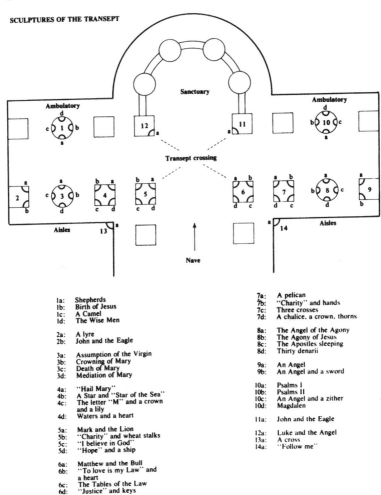

SCULPTURES OF THE TRANSEPT

1a: Shepherds	7a: A pelican
1b: Birth of Jesus	7b: "Charity" and hands
1c: A Camel	7c: Three crosses
1d: The Wise Men	7d: A chalice, a crown, thorns
2a: A lyre	8a: The Angel of the Agony
2b: John and the Eagle	8b: The Agony of Jesus
	8c: The Apostles sleeping
3a: Assumption of the Virgin	8d: Thirty denarii
3b: Crowning of Mary	
3c: Death of Mary	9a: An Angel
3d: Mediation of Mary	9b: An Angel and a sword
4a: "Hail Mary"	10a: Psalms I
4b: A Star and "Star of the Sea"	10b: Psalms II
4c: The letter "M" and a crown and a lily	10c: An Angel and a zither
4d: Waters and a heart	10d: Magdalen
5a: Mark and the Lion	11a: John and the Eagle
5b: "Charity" and wheat stalks	
5c: "I believe in God"	12a: Luke and the Angel
5d: "Hope" and a ship	13a: A cross
	14a: "Follow me"
6a: Matthew and the Bull	
6b: "To love is my Law" and a heart	
6c: The Tables of the Law	
6d: "Justice" and keys	

One of the capitals in the Basilica: the angel and the lyre

In this carving, executed by the combined talents of Émile Brunet and Maurice Lord, the work of the stone-carver is clearly revealed. One can discern how various strokes of the chisel have produced light and shadow effects that enhance the relief. (Photo Moderne) to such an extend that he cannot find two perfectly identical small capitals throughout the whole Basilica.

It is so with the ornamental motifs and arabesques running along the arches; they vary, as it were, to infinity. Albert Mercier had carved the wooden models used by the sculptors of the decorative capitals.

The diagram given above can help identify every subject carved in the capitals and the corner works by the artists Émile Brunet and Maurice Lord.

2. The Column-Statues: on the pillars of the transept

Émile Brunet and Maurice Lord have also executed the four column-statues, which decorate the pillars at the crossing of the nave and the transept. This section is paramount for the proclamation of the Word of God. For that reason, the four Evangelists with their animal symbols have been represented in the vicinity of the pulpit and the ambos. In February 1959, these four giant Indiana stone statues were put in place.

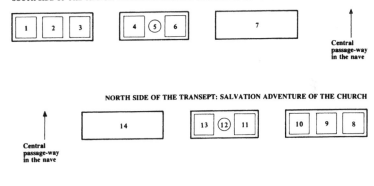

SOUTH SIDE OF THE TRANSEPT: THE SALVATION ADVENTURE OF GOD'S PEOPLE

Central passage-way in the nave

NORTH SIDE OF THE TRANSEPT: SALVATION ADVENTURE OF THE CHURCH

Central passage-way in the nave

South Side of the Transept

1. Abraham leaves Ur, his country
2. Isaac climbs Mount Moriah
3. Jacob's Dream
4. The Hebrews cross the Red Sea
5. Medallion: portrait of Moses
6. The Hebrews in the desert
7. Celebration of the Passover in the desert

North Side of the Transept

8. The calling of the Apostles Peter and Andrew
9. The calling of the Apostles Philip and Nathanael
10. The College of the Apostles
11. Paul's preaching in Corinth
12. Medallion: Portrait of Jesus
13. Peter's crucifixion
14. A celebration at St. Peter's Square, in Rome

D. The front of the pews:

The pews of the Basilica appear somewhat like an oak fence at the limit of the transept. This long wooden strip is decorated with an array of original reliefs. These wooden carvings were drawn by Father Laurent Proulx, C.Ss.R. and executed by Franz Moroder. For details, please refer to Father Proulx's book: *"The Stalls and Pews in the Basilica of Sainte-Anne-de-Beaupré"*, pages 19 to 26. We give here an enumeration of the subjects developed along the general idea of the *"marvelous history of God's people"* (Loc. cit. p. 20).

E. The pavement of the transept:

The pavement of the transept is entirely made up of mosaic tiles and was executed by Walter del Mistro. A lengthly explanation of this decoration is given on pages 15 to 19 of the book: *"The Mosaic Pavements of Saint Ann's Basilica"*, by Father Laurent Proulx, C.Ss.R.

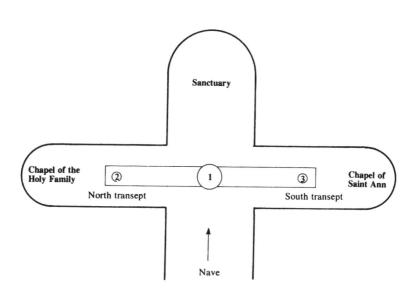

The mosaic pavement in the middle of the transept extends like five carpets, two of which display a harmony of decorative arabesques. The other three carpets picture spiritual realities, which influence the history of salvation as related in the Bible.

1. **The tree of Eden:** It is right in the middle of the transept at the entrance of the sanctuary. This symbol was taken from the Book of Genesis.

2. **The Gate of Heaven:** A gate where many roads converge stands out behind a tree personifying Christ. It is on the north side of the transept.

3. **The infernal monster:** A personage who haunts the pages of the Bible and appears as the embodiment of Evil, that God has to keep at bay constantly. It is in a medallion on the left side of the transept.

F. The chapels of the transept:

There is an apsidal chapel at either end of the transept. Each of them is flanked with two lateral altars. On the south side, stands the chapel of the Holy Family, flanked, on the left, by the altar of Francis of Assisi and, on the right, by the altar of Our Lady of Sorrows. On the north side, is the chapel of the Great Relic, behind the miraculous statue in that section of the church which many people like to call "Saint Ann's Shrine". This chapel extends to the altar of the Holy Curé of Ars on the left and to the altar of the Holy Canadian Martyrs on the right.

A. The Chapel of the Holy Family:

In 1944, Bishop Philippe Desranleau of Sherbrooke declared his diocese's intention to offer to the Shrine a chapel in honor of the Holy Family. At that time, it was impossible to import marble from Italy on account of the War. But, the "Compagnie Canadienne de Carrelages" found in New York a huge block of green marble of the kind commonly called "St-Denis". Since this marble intended for the statue was of a rather light green color, a contrasting "green of the Alps" was chosen for the marble pilasters. The execution of the stained glass windows was to be entrusted to the best glass-painter who would be chosen to produce all the stained glass window of the Basilica. Auguste Labouret won the contest and the three stained glass windows of the chapel were executed by him: in the middle, the Eternal Father; at his left, Saint Joachim among his sheep; at his right, Saint Ann with a ship below her feet. On the panels between the windows are pictured the coat of arms of the Sherbrooke diocese (St. Michael) and the arms of Bishop Desranleau.

A statue of the Holy Family was first carved by Louis Sorbonne. In 1976, the year the Basilica was consecrated, Sherbrooke's Archibishop, Jean-Marie Fortier, who dedicated the chapel, requested that Sorbonne's statue be removed and replaced by Louis Jobin's group, which had been placed outside in the square of the Basilica. The altar-table and the credence are of polished black granite adorned with gold and with mosaic decorations. The retable is made of chipped glass tiles with a gold background, partly spangled with crosses. On Bishop Desranleau's special request, the vault represents the Holy Spirit handing out his gifts:

"The mosaic vault would be nice if the decoration could be centered on a representation of the Holy Spirit in the form of a dove, with his seven gifts as radiating beams of light spreading out over the Holy Family". (Letter dated November 20, 1945, ASA, B-10b, b. 1/doc. 19 901).

Auguste Labouret conceived this mosaic vault in tones of yellow tending to gold, and the work was executed by "La Compagnie Canadienne de Carrelages".

The chapel of the Holy Family is where the Christmas crib is set up in the Basilica. At Sainte-Anne-de-Beaupré, the Christmas crib is unique, since all the figures are life-size and made of polychrome wood. The personages were carved jointly by Louis Jobin and Franz Moroder. The personages are dressed in the manner of Spanish statues. According to tradition, Saint Ann, Jesus' Grandmother, always stands among the personages of the crib at Sainte-Anne-de-Beaupré. Father Laurent Proulx, C.Ss.R., in his book: *"The Christmas Crib at Saint Ann's Basilica"*, (70 pages), tells the story of this crib. The book is on sale at the Pilgrimage Office.

During the pilgrimage season, the Chapel of the Holy Family is the place where the *banners* are put away after being used in the candlelight processions. Many of those banners have been donated by groups and associations that gather here every pilgrimage season. At the Holy Family chapel, are also kept *two procession statues* of Saint Ann, one big, the other small. They are placed on a base furnished with shafts so as to be carried on the shoulders of four bearers. The one used most of the time in processions was carved in 1941 by Angers of Quebec. It is of soft wood so as to be lighter to carry. It was painted by the Sisters of the Good Shepherd, in their Quebec workshop, under the direction of Sister St-Amédée.

B. The Altars of **Francis of Assisi** and of **Our Lady of Sorrows**

These two altars are *similar* to those flanking the Great Relic, at the north end of the transept. All these altars stand under a molded cornice and are framed in a decoration of polished black granite from Alma, ornamented with thin streaks of gold. Their dimensions are the same, namely six feet for the altar-table and seven feet for the retable with cut-off corners.

a. The Altar of Saint Francis of Assisi:

Located on the left of the Holy Family chapel, it stands near the first steps on the stairs leading to the ambulatory around the sanctuary. The altar-table is of black "petit granit", ornamented with a wavy decorative line and carved knobs. The support of the altar is a block of Alpine green granite, flanked by two columns and bearing a monogram: the letters S.F.A. stand for Francis of Assisi. There is also the Latin inscription: "Moriar, Domine, amore amoris tui", which means: "May I die from the love aroused by your love". These words of Saint Francis of Assisi also explain the group of white Carrara marble placed on the altar. Reminiscent of a painting by the Spanish artist Murillo, the scene follows the mystic tradition according to which Saint Francis of Assisi shows so much compassion for Christ that he becomes able to take Him down from the cross. The group was carved in 1950 by the firm A.S. Henreaux de Querceta of Italy. Above this statue, there is a sculptured tympanum, which, in conception and execution, is entirely the work of sculptor Maurice Lord. The scene represents Christ appearing to Saint Francis in the form of a seraph with opened wings and marking the saint's body with stigmata. The event took place on Mount Alverne. The altar of Saint Francis of Assisi was offered by Father John Mickum of Reading, Pennsylvania.

b. *The Altar of Our Lady of Sorrows:*

Standing on the right of the Holy Family chapel and making a pair with the altar of Saint Francis of Assisi, the altar of Our Lady of Sorrows is near the stairs leading to the crypt. The altar-table is made of polished black "petit granit" from Belgium. The altar-support is of forest green marble with contrasting veins. The retable is a panel of forest green marble in a frame of black Belgium marble. It bears the Latin inscription: "Pro peccatis suae gentis, vidit Jesus in tourmentis", meaning: "For the sins of his race, she saw Jesus suffering". These words were taken from the hymn "Sabat Mater", which is recited on the feast of Our Lady of Sorrows. The sculptured group on this altar was executed by the same firm as that on the altar of Saint Francis of Assisi. The carved tympanum is also a work of Maurice Lord. It evokes this most important moment in the Virgin's life when she stood at the foot of the cross near her dying son, Jesus. The chapel was offered by Father Francis Hoffman, the Christian Women and the Knights of Columbus of Pittsburgh, Pennsylvania.

C. The Chapel of the Great Relic:

As soon as the summer of 1943, it was decided to finish the chapel of the Great Relic. Since it was the most important in the Basilica, it was to be beautiful and magnificent.

This chapel was conceived in relation to the *central triptych* with Saint Ann's statue. In order to secure the proper materials, architect Louis-N. Audet, accompanied by Jean Adams of "La Compagnie Canadienne de Carrelages" to which the execution of the chapel had been commissioned, went to Europe to choose the materials and the necessary craftsmen. The "Compagnie Canadienne de Carrelages" contacted two

European firms for the execution of the work: the firm Henraux de Querceta of Lucci, Italy and the firm Merbès-Sprimont of Bruxelles. In Italy, Audet, met Leone Tommazi of Pietrasanta who was to carve the triptych, namely a statue flanked by two panels. The statue represents Saint Ann with the Virgin on her right arm. Above her, an Angel is about to crown her, and four other Angels hold a streamer with three inscriptions, two in French, one in Latin: "All Hail Saint Ann!", "Protect your Children", "Praise Saint Ann". The panel on the left, pictures Saint Ann rescuing distressed seamen. The panel on the right shows the cure of Louis Guimond, the first pilgrim to be miraculously cured at Sainte-Anne-de-Beaupré. The inscriptions in French mean: "Saint Ann, Heaven for the Shipwrecked" and "Beaupré, Land of Miracles". The Latin inscriptions are the following: on the left: "Be our strength in the morning" and on the right: "And our salvation in time of hardships". The two panels are of white marble, but the statue of Saint Ann is made of yellow Balentino marble. The Virgin's robe is inlaid with lapis lazuli decorations. The triptych rests on a strip of stylized acanthus leaves. At the foot of the triptych, stands Saint Ann's reliquary, which will be described later.

The altar-table is made of polished black granite with a fine stripe of dentils along the front and the sides. The table rests on six green onyx pilasters from Brazil. They are 14 inches wide with two narrow shaped ornamental grooves. In the center of the support, the words "Good Saint Ann, pray for us" are inscribed within a square framed in panels of carved maple leaves. The altar step is of red stalagmitic marble with decorations of red, yellow and black marble. The floor of the chapel is paved with red marble tiles, separated by rectangles of black marble. The wall is coated with stalagmitic marble and ornamented with Mexican onyx columns from Padrana. The columns are four feet, six inches high. The capitals topping these columns were carved by Leone Tommazi of Pietrasanta, Italy. The onyx was supplied by Merbès-Sprimont Co. of Bruxelles: fourteen octagonal columns and eight round ones hewn from two onyx blocks that had been stored at the company's workshop near Bruxelles. On each side of the chapel, there is a credence made of the same marble as that of the wall coating. The stained glass windows, made by Auguste Labouret, represent Pope *Leo XIII* who gave the church of Saint-Ann the title of Basilica, *Bishop de Laval,* the first Bishop of Quebec and *Cardinal Taschereau,* the first Canadian Cardinal, who together with the latter, was an ardent promoter of the devotion to Saint Ann. The wall surface behind the heating system radiators, is covered with panels of red-veined Moroccan marble. Two panels of stalagmitic marble bear the engraved names of all the dioceses which belong to the Quebec archdiocese and which have contributed to the completion of the chapel: Rimouski, Gaspé, Golfe Saint-Laurent, Labrador, Quebec, Three-Rivers, Chicoutimi, Nicolet, Amos. The arms of these dioceses appear in the stained glass windows.

The chapel is vaulted like the cavity of an ancient baking oven and is decorated with a mosaic by Auguste Labouret. At the top, the Eternal Father, then Saint Ann who spreads her large coat as if to protect the pilgrims, the sick and certain personages who have played an important role in expanding the devotion to Saint Ann in this century: Father *Jean Tielen,* one of the first Belgian Redemptorists to work at the Shrine, *Father Lamontagne,* who researched Saint Ann's history, *Brother Camille,* sacristan at the former Basilica and *Mother Marie-Anne,* foundress of the Sisters of Saint Ann.

The communion rail is of stalagmitic marble; it is equipped with copper gates bearing monograms of Saint Ann.

Saint Ann's Relic and Reliquary:

The point of interest at Saint Ann's chapel is the famous relic, commonly called the Great Relic. Almost all the relics of Saint Ann in the world have come from the Shrine of Sainte-Anne-d'Apt in Provence, but some of them have been venerated in Rome, namely at the Basilica of Saint-Paul-Outside-the-Walls. At Sainte-Anne-de-Beaupré, there are several relics of Saint Ann, as can be seen during the solemn veneration of the relic after the evening procession. The first relic had been donated by Bishop de Laval himself and, for a long time, the pilgrims had venerated the so-called "Great Relic", brought from

Saint Ann's Great Relic
The Great Relic is on the altar of Saint Ann's chapel. This forearm of Jesus' Grandmother was donated to the Shrine by Pope John XXIII on July 3, 1960. (Photograph by René Baillargeon)

Rome by Mgr Callixte Marquis and donated to the Shrine by Cardinal Taschereau. The one that is now exposed for veneration is Saint Ann's forearm, brought from the Basilica of Saint-Paul-Outside-the-Walls and donated to the Shrine by Pope John XXIII on July 3, 1960. The relic is encased in an *arm of gold,* which is itself enclosed in a reliquary. This reliquary was made at the Maredsous Abbey under the direction of Dom Braum, o.s.b. It is of gilt copper and the front part, framing the glass pane, is decorated with strips of blue enamel, inlaid with streams of carved maple leaves and linked together by motifs with an onyx knob in the center.

On the sides, there are six medallions picturing the following scenes: on the left side, "Saint Ann's dream", "Saint Ann praying", "The meeting at the Golden Gate", and on the right side, "The Virgin's birth", "The Virgin's education", "Two seamen praying at the feet of Saint Ann". In these enamels, the personages are represented in the national clothes of Brittany, France. The base of the reliquary bears three inscriptions: on the front: "O Good Saint Ann" and on the sides: "Fertile Mother" and "Stout Woman".

On the altar stands a crucifix flanked by four brass candlesticks, studded with bits of onyx and made also at Maredsous after Louis-N. Audet's plans.

D. The Altars of the **Holy Curé of Ars** and of the **Holy Canadian Martyrs:**

a. The Altar of the Holy Curé of Ars:

The altar table is made of black Belgian "petit granit" and the support is of Moroccan onyx bearing two leaves with contrasting veins separated by carved strips inlaid with mosaic decorations. The base of the support is of black Belgian marble. The pedestal on which rests the statue of the Holy Priest of Ars, is made of red stalagmitic granite: the statue is of polychrome stucco. The Latin inscription: "Animam meam pono pro ovibus meis" means: "I offer my life for my sheep" and points to Saint John Vianney's pastoral zeal. The carved tympanum is by Maurice Lord, who conceived the scene and carved it out of

Indiana stone; Saint John Vianney is pictured as a priest exercising his pastoral zeal. This chapel has been offered to the Shrine by the priests of Quebec.

b. The Altar of the Holy Canadian Martyrs:

This altar is almost identical to the one on the left side of the Great Relic chapel. It stands in the north transept, near the steps leading to the ambulatory. The altar-table is of black "petit granit". The support is made of two slabs of red Moroccan onyx between two red stalagmitic pilasters. Various mosaic ornaments and different sculptures decorate the support of the altar and the sides of the table. The pedestal on which rests the white marble statue is of antique red marble. The altar is dedicated to the Canadian Martyrs, but the decoration memorializes one of them almost exclusively. It is Saint Jean de Brébeuf who has been embodied in the statue and it is also his martyrdom that has been portrayed in the tympanum by Maurice Lord. The Latin inscription is Tertullian's saying: "The Blood of Martyrs is a Seed of Christians". The chapel has been donated by Colonel Oscar Gilbert.

E. The Miraculous Statue:

In front of the altar of the Great Relic, in the north arm of the transept, stands the miraculous statue at a well-known spot of the Shrine; people come in crowds to pray at the foot of the monumental statue of the Basilica's patron Saint. The story of this statue is worth knowing.

The first miraculous statue was blessed on the 20th of July of 1881, at the 7 o'clock parochial high Mass. This statue of polychrome wood had been made at the Gand workshop of Mathias Zens, a Munich Academy student belonging to the German school of sculpture in Overbeck. The statue had been donated by the family of Father Hendricks, one of the Belgian Redemptorists serving at Sainte-Anne-de-Beaupré. (ABSA, 1881, p. 124)

At the special request of Father Nicolas Mauron, Superior General of the Redemptorists, Pope Leo XIII granted the privi-

The great statue inside the Basilica

Made of polychrome wood, the statue stands against a gilt metal glory.
(Photo Moderne)

lege to crown the statue, which amounted to placing a diadem on Saint Ann's head and another on the Virgin's. Leo XIII had specified the crown should be a precious one. (ABSA, 1937, p. 358) The crowning took place on the 14th of September 1887, in the presence of a very large crowd for the time: 10 000 pilgrims and many Bishops among whom Bishops Taschereau and Duhamel. The Virgin was the first to be crowned with a diadem of gold lilies, then Saint Ann received her gold diadem decked with precious stones: amethysts, turquoises and corals.

The two diadems had been made at Van Ryswick's studio in Anvers. Quebec ladies had donated jewels to decorate them. The miraculous statue was saved from the fire on March 1922, but on the night of November 7th 1926, the statue which was standing in the place of honor, in the middle of the chapel, was destroyed by fire with the chapel, in spite of relentless efforts to save it.

On December 11, 1926, Father Véranne, a Redemptorist from Bruxelles, at the request of Saint Ann's custodians, contacted Jules de Vischer, successor to Mathias Zens, to discuss the carving of a new "miraculous statue". Fortunately, the model of the first statue carved in 1881, had been kept at Zen's studio and there was also a well seasoned oak log available. So, by June 18, 1927, the new "miraculous statue" had arrived at the Shrine. It was in every way identical to the first except that it was larger to fit in with the new Basilica. It was eight feet or 2,25 metres high. On July 17, 1927, Bishop Hermann Brunault presided the installation ceremony of the new "miraculous statue" that was placed in the center of the new temporary church arranged in the basement of the Basilica. The statue was carried from the monastery to the Basilica and Bishop Brunault blessed it. In 1929, a pedestal and a glory were added according to Louis-N. Audet's plans. In July 1934, when the upper church was inaugurated after the construction of the floor, the statue was placed, not in the middle of the church as usual, but in the north transept. This was not in accordance with tradition, but it followed liturgical regulations and complied with a wish expressed by Cardinal Rodrigue Villeneuve. The new statue had not been crowned with precious diadems like those of the former statue. So, on October 12, 1958, the statue was crowned with new precious diadems made by Aurelio Hernandez of Quebec.

The pedestal of the statue was sketched by Louis-N. Audet and executed by Daprato Co. It was installed on February 4, 1929, but the work had taken four years. Here is a list of materials used in the pedestal.

The step riser: Portoro and Breccia Sera Vezza marble

The step tread: Alpine green marble

The balustrade: Sienna marble with Portoro base

The balusters: white, antique green and Verona marbles decked with mosaics

The pedestal panels: Orient pink marble

The arches: pure white statuary marble

The pillar: Italian onyx

The capital: brass

On April 20, 1928, E. Saint-Aubin of Robert Mitchell C. of Montreal was commissioned to make the glory, namely a composition of straight and flamboyant rays of gold to be put against the back of the statue. (SAS, B-10a, b, 2/doc. 13 435)

It is worthy of notice that the present statue respects the iconographic tradition of Sainte-Anne-de-Beaupré, which for a century has represented Saint Ann with the Virgin on her right arm and her forefinger pointing to the sky. Other traditions represent her in the reverted posture.

7. THE SANCTUARY OF THE BASILICA

(Following the explanations given on the transept, the careful observation of each element being described has no doubt led you away from your original observation spot. We suggest now that you return to that spot, namely the medallion of the Tree of Eden, for the explanation on the sanctuary).

The sanctuary is the area confined by the communion rail and the black-based column of the apse. This area is 65 feet long and 45 feet wide, that is, 19,6 metres by 13,7 metres. Until 1948, the sanctuary contained little more than a very simple altar surrounded by temporary pews arranged in a hemicycle, opening more or less on the ambulatory. The finishing of the sanctuary began on August 11, 1947, with the signing of the first contract between the Shrine's custodians and Collet Brothers Co. of Montreal. The work took three years with the summer interruptions and included the stone coating of the walls, the triforium and the eighteen columns and pillars.

The stone of the walls is Texas Travertine (or Cordova) and that of the columns and other carved architectural elements is Indiana stone.

"It was not an easy task to cut, at the factory, all the stone, the arches, the columns, which had to perfectly fit the already made vault and even the carved cornice that separated the wall from the vault. That work, perhaps the most important ever undertaken in Canada, was executed by Martineau Freestone Co. of Montreal, with the help of Mr. Forest, engineer for Collet & Brothers, as coordinator of the indoor work. Forest relied on the indispensable cooperation of Mr. Joseph Danis, a real geometry genius, who marked out the exact cut of each stone. Mr. Danis put all his heart into his work, to such an extent that he died of exhaustion. Saint Ann had completely charmed his heart. Even on his deathbed, he was heard recommending special attention to the arches of the sanctuary». (Louis-N. Audet, ASA, B-10a, b.14/doc. 17 781, p. 8)

A. THE VAULT OF THE SANCTUARY:

The apsidal vault over the sanctuary of the Basilica is the extension and the most conspicuous part of the great barrel vault of the nave. For that reason, its decoration was intended to glorify Saint Ann, to whom the Basilica had been dedicated. The decoration work was commissioned to Auguste Labouret who, after having long debated the suitable size and posture of the personages, chose to supervise himself the laying of the vault mosaic in the spring of 1940. All that one might want to know about the mosaic of the sanctuary in thoroughly

Detail of the interior of the Basilica

This part of the sanctuary shows how, at the Basilica, different techniques have been combined and harmonized to produce a strikingly sumptuous and beautiful finish: stone carving, stained glass, mosaic, wrought-iron lattice and woodwork. (Photograph by Luc) explained in the following book by Father Laurent Proulx, C.Ss.R., especially on pages 66 to 71: *"The Central Arch in the Basilica of Sainte-Anne-de-Beaupré"*. Here are only a few general notes that may help interpret this vast tableau offering a view into Heaven, where Saint Ann is being glorified.

There are three fields of glorification:

1. Saint Ann and the Mystery of the Holy Trinity

On a vertical line, the Eternal Father is seen holding, in his left hand, the symbol of his creative power, the globe and making a blessing gesture with his right hand. The Holy Spirit stands between the Father and the Infant-Jesus, the Incarnate Word. Two Angels, hands joined, bow in adoration. On a horizontal line, three earthly generations are pictured: Ann, the grandmother on the right; Mary, the daughter, on the left and, in the middle, the divine Infant holding an apple, which symbolizes man's original disobedience.

2. The Procession of the Elect:

The saints and patron of the Canadian Church pay homage to Saint Ann:

North Side:
St. John, the Baptizer, patron saint of French speaking Canadians,
St. Joseph, St. Ann's son-in-law and Canada's patron saint,
St. Isaac Jogues, a Jesuit and Canadian martyr,
St. Charles Garnier, a Jesuit and Canadian martyr,
St. Jean de la Lande, a Jesuit and Canadian martyr,
St. René Goupil, a Jesuit and Canadian martyr,
Blessed Marguerite Bourgeois, foundress of the Notre-Dame Sisters, Kateri Tekakwita, Iroquois virgin,
Venerable Mary of the Incarnation, foundress of the Ursulines of Quebec, one of the first witnesses to talk about Sainte-Anne-du-Petit-Cap,
The Servant of God, Alfred Pampalon, a Redemptorist, whose remains are preserved in a reliquary in the crypt.

South Side:

St. Joachim, Saint Ann's husband,
Bishop François de Montmorency Laval, first Bishop of North America and famous promoter of the devotion to Saint Ann,
St. Gabriel Lalement, a Jesuit and Canadian martyr,
St. Jean de Brébeuf, a Jesuit and Canadian martyr,
St. Antoine Daniel, a Jesuit and Canadian martyr,
St. Noël Chabanel, a Jesuit and Canadian martyr,
Mother Marie-Rose, foundress of the Sisters o the Holy Names of Jesus and Mary,
Blessed Marguerite d'Youville, foundress of the sisters of Charity,
Brother Didace Pelletier, a Recollet, first child to be inscribed in the baptism register of the Sainte-Anne-du-Petit-Cap's parish in 1657.

3. The Choirs of the Angels:

Between the transverse arches separating the sanctuary from the transept, there is a vault section entirely set apart for the Angels who sing praise to the accompaniment of musical instruments. This tableau is reminiscent of Fra Angelico's creations. Two adoring Angels rise above the six musicians.

B. THE STAINED GLASS WINDOWS IN THE SANCTUARY:

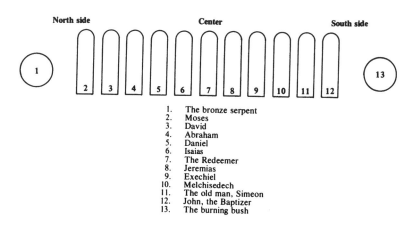

1. The bronze serpent
2. Moses
3. David
4. Abraham
5. Daniel
6. Isaias
7. The Redeemer
8. Jeremias
9. Exechiel
10. Melchisedech
11. The old man, Simeon
12. John, the Baptizer
13. The burning bush

The stained glass window of the sanctuary cut into the lower part of the mosaic vault in a series of alcoves that appear like a fringe of iridescent light at the border of the vault. Those stained glass windows were made of chipped glass set in concrete by August Labouret. Two iconographic programs are developed here. At the meeting point of the sanctuary and the transept, there are two bull's-eyes picturing symbols or figures of the Messiah. The eleven single windows crowning the sanctuary with a kaleidoscope of colors, depict the saints of the Old Testament, *the prophets and the patriarchs,* who have lived in the expectation of the Redeemer and who stand out in the brilliant galaxy of the Old Testament saints.

C. THE TRIFORIUM:

The description of the triforium has already been given in this guidebook, but let us add here a few remarks of interest. It is in the sanctuary that the graceful shafts arrayed along this arcaded storey produce their most beautiful architectural effects. The visitor will also like to contemplate the varied and harmonious decoration of the arches that rest on the ten columns and the two pillars of the sanctuary. In the hemicycle of the sanctuary, there are eleven arches resting on the columns and two larger ones resting on the pillars.

Moreover, to decorate the wall space between the arches and the triforium, 12 ornamental crosses were fixed on the Cordova stone: 8 straight crosses and 4 Saint Andrew's crosses. Similar crosses are seen elsewhere in the Basilica, but, in the sanctuary, the motif is more compact and more easily perceived. Between the cornice bordering the vault and the triforium, there are also French inscriptions, which are the most cherished in the Basilica, because they remind the pilgrims of Saint Ann's titles to endless trust and veneration. These invocations were taken from the litanies to Saint Ann:

"Mother of Mary"; "Solace for spouses"; "Assistance to Mothers"; "Bulwark of the Church"; "Mother of the country"; "Hope for seamen"; "Solace for the afflicted; "Mighty Patroness".

D. THE SCULPTURES OF THE CAPITALS:

There are ten columns around the sanctuary. The artists who wanted to produce a stone Gospel had therefore an ample opportunity to exercise their creative talent. We have in the sanctuary a few of the best capitals executed by clay-modeler Émile Brunet and stone-carver Maurice Lord. The pillars are simply decorated with carved corner works.

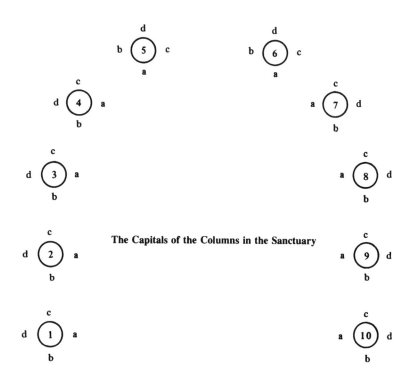

The Capitals of the Columns in the Sanctuary

1a: The Virgin's Betrothal	6a: The Last Supper I
1b: The Presentation	6b: The Last Supper II
1c: An Angel and a lily	6c: The Last Supper III
1d: A Dove scratching for food	6d: The Last Supper IV

2a: The Annunciation	7a: The Wedding Feast at Cana I
2b: The Virgin with a distaff	7b: The Baptism of Jesus
2c: The Virgin's Visitation	7c: The Wedding Feast at Cana II
2d: Joseph, the vine-dresser	7d: Peter fails to walk on water
3a: The flight into Egypt	8a: The Good Shepherd
3b: Joseph and a donkey	8b: Jesus and the man born blind
3c: The massacre of the Innocents I	8c: The Transfiguration
3d: The massacre of the Innocents II	8d: The Samaritan woman
4a: Jesus in the Temple	9a: The prodigal Son
4b: Mary and Joseph in search of Jesus	9b: Jesus calms a storm
4c: The Doctors of the Law	9c: The daughter of Jairus
4d: The Tables of the Law	9d: The Good Samaritan
5a: The multiplication of the loaves I	10a: Psalms I
5b: The sower	10b: Psalms II
5c: The multiplication of the loaves II	10c: Magdalen
5d: Jesus, the worker	10d: An angel with a zither

E. THE MAIN ALTAR AND THE CIBORIUM:

The ensemble made up of the main altar with its tabernacle and its canopy or ciborium, is in the back part of the sanctuary. Both the main altar and the ciborium were made by Fabrico Co., during the fall of 1961 and the first part of the 1962 winter, under the direction of J. Bidegain.

The Ciborium:

It is an octagonal bronze dome resting on six fluted columns made of a nickel and silver alloy. On the top of the ciborium, stands a six-pointed star within a silver circle, which symbolizes Saint Ann. The eight inclines of the dome are decorated with fleur-de-lys and the capitals of the columns are adorned with maple leaves. Bordering the dome, there is a bronze strip studded with precious stones: 72 in all, of which 42 are to be "very precious" and imported from Europe by Mr. d'Henreaux. Here is a list of the stones:

The very precious stones:

6 malachites or green basic carbonates of copper
6 aventurines or light green quartz silicates

6 jaspers or quartz silicates of yellow, red and green colors
6 amethysts or purple quartz silicates
6 agates or transparent quartz
6 antique greens from Greece
6 purple "peach flowers"
The Precious Stones:
6 blacks from Belgium
6 red porphyries from Egypt
6 yellow from Sienna
6 red onyxes from Morocco
6 black onyxes from Pakistan

The Altar:

The altar stands on a triple step of black glazed granite from Alma. The altar-support is of white marble, with carved leaf-scrolls bearing grapevine motifs: leaves, clusters and stems. In the middle of the support, there is a medallion picturing Christ rising from the dead. The whole support is decked with gold. The altar-table, made of black so-called Guernett granite, is 10 feet, 6 inches long and 5 feet, 4 inches wide. A Latin inscription recalls the mystery of Christ's Resurrection: "Dux vitae mortuus, regnat vivus", taken from a hymn to the Blessed Sacrament: "The Master of life, who was dead, now reigns in the fullness of life". There are also a few more traditional symbols of Christ: the Chi and Rho, the Alpha and the Omega, the cross of victory.

The Tabernacle:

The tabernacle now standing on the main altar had been designed for the Blessed Sacrament chapel in the ambulatory. It was made by Albert Gilles of Cowansville in 1950 after Louis-N. Audet's plans. It is 5 feet high and round with a conic dome. It is made of copper, but the wall surface and the doors were plated with gold by Hernandez Co. in February 1978. The copper wall plates are one-quarter of an inch thick and the dome sheet is one-eighth of an inch thick. The interior of the tabernacle is equipped with two independently revolving trays on which can be stored about fifteen ciboriums filled with consecrated hosts for Holy Communion. The front door pictures Isaac's sacrifice and the back door represents Elias in the desert. The four decorative panels bear Eucharistic symbols: manna, two doves quenching their thirst, a pelican and bread with fish. The four Evangelists flank the doors and a globe tops the dome.

The Curtains:

Between the columns in the back of the sanctuary, hangs a curtain, forming a large screen of the season's liturgical color. Behind this curtain, there are three others, each representing a different liturgical color. Thanks to an ingenious mechanism, any of the white, red, green or purple curtains can be quickly exposed according to the needs of the Liturgy.

F. THE GRILLES OF THE SANCTUARY:

The sanctuary is separated from the ambulatory by metal grilles which provide a beautiful decoration as well as a quiet atmosphere of prayer in the sanctuary. The grilles were installed in 1965 by Fabrico Industries, under the supervision of Jean Bidegain. Jean Bidegain drew the plans and Pierre Langlade executed the work. Bidegain spent weeks perfecting the drawings, then the model sculptures were executed at the workshop by Mr. Lemay. P. Langlade prepared the casting molds after the model sculptures, and bronze was cast into them. Once out of the molds, the bronze motifs were bearded off and the reliefs retouched with graving tools.

The decoration program called for the representation of the *floral emblems* of each Canadian Province, within ornamental circles and ellipses. The back door of the sanctuary displays the arms of the Province of Quebec and of the Archdiocese of Quebec. It is a known fact that Saint Ann was declared, in 1876, Patron Saint of the civil and ecclesiastical provinces of Quebec. Here are the floral emblems represented in the grilles of the sanctuary:

Quebec: Madonna lily
Ontario: White trillium
Manitoba: Pasqueflower
Nova-Scotia: Mayflower

New-Brunswick: Marsh blue violet
Prince-Edward-Island: Mocassin flower (stemless lady's slipper)
Alberta: Prairie rose
Saskatchewan: Prairie lily (orange cup)
Newfoundland: Pitcher plant
Yukon: Narrow-leaf primrose
Northwestern Territories: Full-flower water lily

G. THE STALLS IN THE SANCTUARY:

The stalls with a seating capacity of 61 people, were put in place in 1962, at the beginning of winter. The woodwork of quarter-sawed white oak was executed by Deslauriers Co. All the details are given in the following book by Father Laurent Proulx, C.Ss.R.: *"The Stalls and Pews in the Basilica of Sainte-Anne-de-Beaupré"*, more specifically on pages 1 to 13.

There is a triple iconographic program realized here:

a. The *floral emblems* of the Canadian Provinces displayed in the metal grilles are repeated here on the back of the stalls.

b. The *carved medallions* on the front of the prayer-stools bear inscriptions from the litanies to Saint Ann.

c. The stalls are crowned by an array of *small wooden statues.* The Statues portray 50 personages, who have had something to do with the devotion to Saint Ann since the first centuries.

For the details on those sculptures, please refer to Father Proulx's book which explains every chosen symbol. The pertinent research and the sketches were done by Father François Forté, C.Ss.R. and architect Julien Dallaire; all the carvings were executed by sculptor Franz Moroder from Tyrol.

H. THE COMMUNION RAIL AND THE PULPIT:

The sanctuary is separated from the nave by the communion rail which runs along the front part of the platform between the nave and the steps of the sanctuary. From this platform, which is only one step high, and is often called the "lower choir", there are five steps leading up to the sanctuary. The communion rail and the pulpit were installed in 1958 by Aurelio Hernandez of the Spanish Craftsman Co. and by Lucchesi of the Baretti firm, according to the plans drawn by architect Louis-N. Audet.

The Communion Rail:

The communion rail extends to a length of 118 feet. This long line of austere sumptuousness is divided in four sections by five double gates counting the end ones. The step tread is of perlitic marble and the riser is of black Belgian marble. The table of the communion rail is of bracken light dawn marble, braced at both ends by blocks of green St-Denis marble. It is supported all along by a system of twin columns, alternating with blocks of bracken light dawn marble, decked with gold mosaics. The columns are of two different kinds of marble. Of the 18 columns in each section, ten are of red Morrocan onyx and eight of green St-Denis marble, for a total of 72 columns, topped with decorative white marble capitals.

The Pulpit:

The pulpit stands against the first pillar on the south side of the sanctuary with a flight of stairs on each side. The pulpit proper is of white Carrara marble, with a top and a bottom strip of bracken light dawn marble. It is supported by two sturdy columns of green St-Denis marble. The balustrade rests on two pillars of Moroccan onyx, each decorated with an acanthus. An Angel of white Carrara marble supports the console.

I. THE PAVEMENT OF THE SANCTUARY:

Father Laurent Proulx's book: *"The Mosaic Pavement of Saint Ann's Basilica"* describes the pavement of the sanctuary on pages 21 and 22. Here are a few brief observations:

a. The Lower-Choir:

The area between the communion rail and the stairs of the sanctuary is called the lower-choir. It is paved with a system of marble slabs alternating with decorative strips.

At this moment of the visit, you may have noticed that some

furnishings in the sanctuary are still temporary: the crucifix of the main altar, the seat of the officiating priest, the procession cross, the ambos and the altar where Mass is celebrated facing the congregation. A few years from now, visitors will probably find changes in the furnishings of the sanctuary.

b. The Stairs of the Sanctuary:

The stairs are 14 feet wide and the five steps are made of perlitic marble with risers of black Belgium marble.

c. The Pavement in the Sanctuary:

There are three elements here: a central carpet, two decorative strips, one on each side, and a narrow border all around.

8. THE APSE OF THE BASILICA

(We suggest now that you head toward the north side, pass between the miraculous statue and the communion rail, climb the steps leading to the ambulatory and walk as far as the intersection opposite Our Lady's chapel).

In the apse of the Basilica, you find mainly two things: *a vast ambulatory or walkway* around the sanctuary and a series of *radiating chapels.*

A. THE AMBULATORY:

1. The Vaults:

The ambulatory vaulting is rather capricious. In the section parallel to the transept, there are groined vaults; at the intersection of the transept and the ambulatory proper, there are two small cupolas, one on each side, and finally, all around the sanctuary, there is that long curving barrel vault notched on one side by the arches of the chapels and, on the other side, by the arches of the sanctuary. For a complete explanation of the decorative technique used on the vaults, please look up pages 3 to 8 of Father Laurent Proulx's book: *"The Secondary Vaults in the Basilica of Sainte-Anne-de-Beaupré".*

The ornamentation of the vaults was commissioned to Jean

Gaudin, who in 1949, decided to decorate them with stoneware arabesque set off by gold tones. Walter del Mistro supervised the laying of the mosaics, which had been prepared in a Paris workshop. These vaults are supposed to be, as it were, a link between the stained glass windows, the wall mosaics of the ambulatory and the sanctuary. Jean Gaudin has unrolled a discreet ornamentation based on light ochers set off by grays and golds.

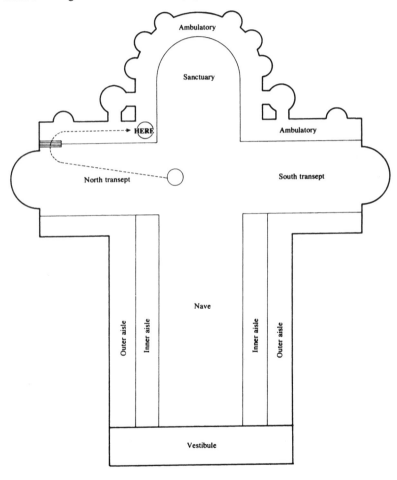

2. The Stained Glass Windows of the Ambulatory:

There are four systems of stained glass windows in the ambulatory.

1. The Bull's Eyes:

These two windows, near the pillars, make a pair with those in the transept: they portray the Evangelists Saint Luke and Saint Matthew

2. The Twin Windows of the Ambulatory: the Gallery of the Apostles.

As for the twin windows mentioned above, the 14 stained glass windows of this gallery were produced at Auguste Larouret's workshop in Paris. They are made of superbly colored glass embedded in concrete. At Sainte-Anne-de-Beaupré, 14 personages are portrayed in the gallery of the Apostles: the eleven members of the Apostolic College as it was after Judas' betrayal, Saint Matthias who was elected by the eleven as Judas' successor, Saint Paul who by a special calling from God was chosen as the Apostle of the Gentiles and, finally, Saint Barnabas who was Paul's first companion.

3. The Small Stained Glass Windows between the Radiating Chapels:

Between the six radiating chapels around the sanctuary, there are four stained glass windows made of rather thin glass

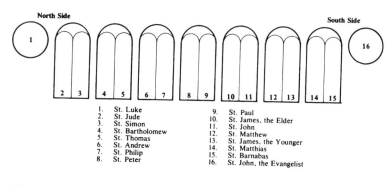

1. St. Luke	9. St. Paul
2. St. Jude	10. St. James, the Elder
3. St. Simon	11. St. John
4. St. Bartholomew	12. St. Matthew
5. St. Thomas	13. St. James, the Younger
6. St. Andrew	14. St. Matthias
7. St. Philip	15. St. Barnabas
8. St. Peter	16. St. John, the Evangelist

cased in lead strips. Though he didn't favor this technique, Auguste Labouret fabricated them at the special request of the artists entrusted with the decoration of the Basilica; they wanted these stained glass windows and those of the radiating chapels to be of the lead-set type. They represent symbols of Christ's passion: "Crown of Thorns", "Bound Hands", "Nails", "Whips". Labouret added "studs of chipped glass to harmonize these windows with the others made of thick chipped glass set in concrete." (ASA, B-10b, b.1/doc. 20 031)

4. The Stained Glass Windows of *the Radiating Chapels:*

These windows are also made of thin glass set in lead strips; their description will be given with the explanations on the radiating chapels.

B. THE WIDE MOSAIC STRIP ON THE WALL OF THE AMBULATORY:

The wall of the ambulatory was decorated with *a wide mosaic strip* by Auguste Labouret, who began his work in 1947 and finished it in 1951. The entire space between the cornice under the windows and the arches of the radiating chapels has been covered with mosaic from the northwest wall to the southeast wall of the transept. It is an impressively vast surface varying from 8 to 14 feet in width and extending from one end of the ambulatory to the other.

The iconographic program of the mosaic is double. In the part that runs along the transept arms, the mosaic strip depicts some episodes in the lives of the saints whose chapels are below the mosaic. The sections above the chapels of the Lord and of the Virgin, represent their respective salutary action. On the wall of the ambulatory proper, the entire *Eucharistic mystery* is memorialized: its prefiguration, its institution and its effect on the life of the Church.

There are two systems of pictorial arrangements. A series of large rectangular tableaux represent scenes related to the Holy Eucharist. Alternating with these, there is a *sequence of symbols of the same mystery.* There are 13 wide tableaux measuring

OUTER WALL OF THE AMBULATORY

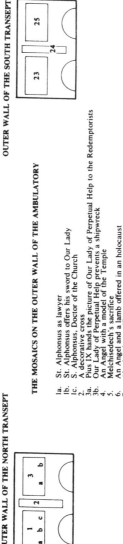

OUTER WALL OF THE SOUTH TRANSEPT

OUTER WALL OF THE NORTH TRANSEPT

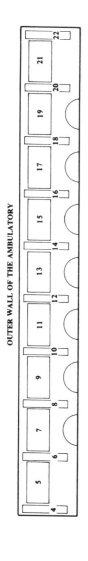

THE MOSAICS ON THE OUTER WALL OF THE AMBULATORY

1a. St. Alphonsus as lawyer
1b. St. Alphonsus offers his sword to Our Lady
1c. S. Alphonsus, Doctor of the Church
2. A decorative cross
3a. Pius IX hands the picture of Our Lady of Perpetual Help to the Redemptorists
3b. Our Lady of Perpetual Help prevents a shipwreck
4. An Angel with a model of the Temple
5. Melchisedech's sacrifice
6. An Angel and a lamb offered in an holocaust
7. Abraham's sacrifice
8. An Angel with wheat stalks
9. Miraculous manna
10. An Angel with loaves of bread
11. The promise of the Eucharist
12. Mary offers her Son to the World
13. The Last Supper
14. The Church offers the bread and wine of life to the World
15. Mass in the Catacombs
16. An Angel with fishes (IXTUS is a symbol of Christ)
17. Saint Tarsicius' martyrdom
18. An Angel and a vineplant and grapes
19. The Blessed Sacrament Procession
20. An Angel offers a cross
21. Saint Pius X and communion for children
22. An Angel with a model of St-Peter's Basilica
23. Christ preaches love to all men: "Come to me all you who are weary and find life burdensome and I will refresh you".
24. A decorative cross
25. Archangel Michael gives communion to young Gerard Majella

18 feet by 6 feet and, counting the two decorative crosses on the transept side, there are 12 symbols, six feet high and three feet wide. The diagram herewith details the chosen subjects. The rather special mosaic technique gives bold relief to the scenes by picturing them on a gold background. Walter del Mistro has decked the gold background with a kind of ceramic embroidery that subtly tempers the glaring effect of the golds and adds to the whole a sense of distinction. Louis-N. Audet wrote to Auguste Labouret what he wanted to see in this decorative strip: "Less richness of tone in the overall aspect of the mosaic, but a more compact design with discreet quadrillé background". (ASA, B-10b, b.i/doc. 19 984, passim) The same Louis-N. Audet expressed his impression when he saw the face of Christ in the Last Supper scene, which, according to Auguste Labouret's assistant, Pierre Chaudière, was executed after the head of the Spanish painter, El Greco. "Did I tell you that I was struck by the figure of Christ in the Last Supper scene? For a long time, I stood contemplating that noble expression, that air of majesty; it is really well done". (ASA, B-10b, b.i/doc. 20 157)

C. THE RADIATING CHAPELS:

All around the ambulatory, the radiating chapels spread like flower petals. Besides enlivening marvelously the ambulatory with their varied and resplendent finish, these chapels make the church apse a pleasant harmony of curves presenting a most beautiful architectural effect. Here is a detailed presentation of the chapels beginning with those of the north transept.

A. THE CHAPEL OF SAINT ALPHONSUS LIGUORI:

This chapel is the first in the ambulatory on the north side and it faces the transept.

The Altar: Because a staircase leading to the crypt occupies the back of the chapel, the altar has been placed in the front part of the chapel.

The Altar-step: The step on which rests the altar is of three tones of yellow marble with a riser of black marble.

The Altar-table: polished black granite.

The Altar-support: a wide panel of green onyx from Brazil, flanked by two columns of green marble.

The Retable: yellow Sienna marble with a strip of mosaic. On both sides of the retable, there are crosier-shaped wrought iron ornaments.

The Statue: the statue tops the white marble tabernacle; it was made at the S. Henreaux workshop, in Italy.

The Chapel:

The Walls: Texas Travertine or Cordova.

The Vault: It is covered with a mosaic by Auguste Labouret. Since the chapel is dedicated to Saint Alphonsus and is also offered by the Redemptorists who are the Shrine's custodians, the mosaic represents the glorification of Saint Alphonsus. The Latin motto: "Et circa illum corona fratrum" means: "And around him a crown of brothers". The founder of the Redemptorists stands on the left surrounded by Angels and, below the arms of the Congregation, is the cross of Redemption. Saint Alphonsus points to his disciples, who have walked the road to holiness; in the first row: Saint Gerard Majella accompanied by an Angel; in the second row: Saint Clement-Mary Hofbauer and Venerable Joseph Armand Passerat; in the third row: Saint John Newmann and the Servant of God, Alfred Pampalon.

The Windows: These windows of lead-set stained glass, made by Auguste Labouret, represent the virtues of Saint Alphonsus in symbols.

Dogma, symbolized by the *pastoral crosier*
Zeal, symbolized by the *Sun* with rays
Prayer, symbolized by a *censer*

The notion around which gravitate all the elements of this chapel is expressed in the Latin text inscribed on the retable: "Evangelizare pauperibus misit me, sanare contritos corde", meaning: "He has sent me to preach the Gospel to the poor, to cure the repentant hearts". The marble work was done by S.

Henreaux Co. and the chapel was realized by the "Compagnie Canadienne de Carrelages". Maxime Roisin, co-architect of the Basilica, on visit in Quebec, drew the plans of the two wrought iron gates and the bronze ornamental work was executed by the Lebrun Brothers of Three-Rivers.

B. THE CHAPEL OF OUR LADY OF PERPETUAL HELP:

The chapel of Our Lady of Perpetual Help, like the Blessed Sacrament chapel, on the south side, is larger than the other chapels in the ambulatory. Placed in the corner at the intersection of the transept and the ambulatory, they also have two openings on the ambulatory. They were both treated with greater attention.

The Virgin of Perpetual Help:

The Redemptorists invoke the Blessed Virgin under the title of Our Lady of Perpetual Help, after an old icon preserved in Saint Alphonsus' church on Via Merulana, Rome. This image has been entrusted to the Redemptorist Fathers by Pope Pius IX, who instructed them to make it known throughout the world. The original image is an icon, namely a painting on a wood panel with a precious aureole around Our Lady's head. This picture occupies the center of the decoration, but it is made of mosaic to fit the marble and mosaic decoration of the chapel. The picture is framed in a Leone Tommasi sculpture, which represents six Angels holding the picture against the wall.

The floor: It is a vast square of gray marble called "Bardiglio", adorned with pieces of black, white, yellow and gray marble. In the corners, there are big yellow lilies of Verona marble.

The Altar: Except for the table of black "petit granit", the altar is made of white Carrara marble decked with sculptures and mosaics. On the altar-support, there are three sculptures portraying Old Testament prototypes of the Virgin: Deborah, Judith and Esther. The tabernacle is adorned with a silver door by Albert Gilles of Cowansville.

The Mosaics: The vault and the two walls of the chapel are covered with mosaics where blues and golds dominate; a work by Jean Gaudin of Paris. The vault is, so to speak, a crown to the Virgin. On the vault pendentives, are pictured symbols of the Blessed Virgin inspired by invocations or excerpts from the Bible:

"The Ark that saves the world".
"She shall crush your head".
"Hail, Star of the sea".
"Like an army ready for battle".

A mosaic serves as a background to the picture of Our Lady of Perpetual Help on the wall behind the altar. On the wall facing the ambulatory, there is a portrait of *Our Lady of Peace,* a title after which the Virgin was invoked during the Ottawa Marian Congress in 1946. Since the chapel was a donation from the Ottawa Archdiocese, Bishop Vachon wanted it to memorialize the Marian Congress. The "Madonna of Peace" stands beside the Cathedral of Ottawa, the Parliament Building, the Repository of the Marian Congress of Ottawa and St. Peter's Basilica of Rome. The names of the dioceses belonging to the Ottawa Archdiocese are inscribed below the image of Our Lady of Peace, a little above the radiator hood of white marble and gold mosaic: James Bay, Timmins, Pembroke, Ottawa, Mont-Laurier.

The Columns: They are of yellow Sienna marble and the capitals are decorated with symbols inspired by the principal invocations in the Litanies of Loretto:

Mystical Rose	Tower of David	On the ambularoty
Seat of Wisdom	Ark of the Covenant	side, the columns
House of Gold	Gate of Heaven	are of *antique*
		red marble.

The Balustrade of the Chapel:

Albert Gilles of Cowansville made the two balustrades and the two gates. He adorned them with 20 copper panels, enhanced with silver. The idea was to display all the different titles after which the Virgin has been invoked throughout the world. Here are the Madonnas portrayed in the panels starting from the north side:

1. Our Lady of LaSalette
2. Our Lady of Lourdes
3. The Immaculate Conception
4. Our Lady of Fatima
5. The Miraculous Medal
6. Our Lady of the Sacred Heart
7. Our Lady of Good Counsel
8. Our Lady of the Holy Rosary
9. Our Lady of Perpetual Help
10. Our Lady of Seven Sorrows

The Relic of Saint Bernadette Soubirous:

In the chapel, there is an ivory reliquary containing a relic of Saint Bernadette Soubirous, the seer of Lourdes. It was donated by Pope Pius XII in 1952.

The Stained Glass Windows: Two small stained glass windows, picturing a dove and lilies, pierce the vault of the chapel. The thick, chipped glass panels set in concrete were made by Auguste Labouret.

The marble, cut by the S. Henreaux firm of Querceta, was laid in Querceta, Italy and the chapel was realized by the "Compagnie Canadienne de Carrelages".

C. THE CHAPEL OF SAINT PATRICK:

In 1946, Father James Cox of Pittsburgh donated a chapel to be dedicated to Saint Patrick. It is the first in the ambulatory near that of the Virgin.

The Floor: It is a system of marble borders: black Belgian marble, yellow Sienna marble, green marble.

The Altar:

The Altar-Step: The altar rest on a step of green St-Denis marble, with inlays of yellow Sienna marble and Verona marble.

The Altar-Table: It is of black "petit granit", adorned with carved clover or shamrock leaves.

The Altar-support: It is of green St-Denis marble inlaid with a large rectangle of yellow marble decorated with a Celtic cross within three concentric circles.

The Triptych: This Peru mahogany sculpture is the work of Sylvia Daoust, a teacher at "Beaux-Arts" of Montreal. In the center, Saint Patrick sits on his episcopal throne; in the left panel, he brings a dead person back to life and, in the right panel, he preaches to Irish folks. The Peru mahogany is touched up with gold and green.

The Walls: They are decorated with two strips of different colors: yellow Verona marble and green St-Denis marble. There are two large panels of St-Denis marble below the windows. The cornice is of Carrara marble with carved clover ornaments.

The Vaults: It is a green-toned mosaic spangled with crosses distributed around a large Nordic cross in the center. There are also several monograms here and there. A long festoon of stylized shamrock leaves borders the vault.

The Windows: Three small lead-set stained glass windows made by Auguste Labouret:

The *World of God,* symbolized by a *sower's hand*
Fortitude, symbolized by a *column*
Praise of God, symbolized by the *harp* as it appears on the Irish flag.

The decoration work of the chapel was executed by Carli-Petrucci Co. of Montreal. The two columns at the entrance to the chapel are of forest green marble.

D. THE CHAPEL OF SAINT JOSEPH:

This chapel was donated to the Shrine by the family of Mr. Philibert Lussier, father of Bishop Philippe Lussier, C.Ss.R., former Bishop of Saint-Paul, Alberta.

The Floor: Most of the pavement is of gray marble, but colored ornaments occupy a comparatively large area: a strip of black marble triangles and another of red marble triangles.

The Altar:

The Altar-step: Rectangles of gray and red marble are framed in a wide border of black marble.

The Altar-Table: It is of glazed light pink Canadian granite.

The Altar-support: It is of red marble and is divided in three sections by two mosaic strips of fleurs-de-lys. In the middle is the Latin inscription: "Justus germinabit sicut lilium et florebit in aeternum, ante Dominum", meaning: "The just shall grow like the lily and blossom eternally in the presence of God".

The Statue: This statue carved out of tulipwood by H. Angers of Quebec, was decorated by the Good Shepherd Sisters of Quebec under the direction of Sister Saint-Amédée. Its pedestal is of light pink granite.

The Walls: They are covered with ten panels of gray marble separated by ornamental bands of small black marble squares alternating with white ones. There is a monogram on the upper part of each panel: Christ, Saint Joseph, The Virgin, Jesus, Mary, Joseph, fleur-de-lys and carpenter tools.

The Vault: It is covered with a mosaic conceived and realized by Walter del Mistro. Above an ornamental band, a vast scene unfolds: the dominant figure is the Holy Spirit, flanked by two Angels with spread out wings; the high priest hands to Saint Joseph a stick, blooming with lily flowers, in a traditional gesture, signifying that God has chosen Saint Joseph to become the spouse of the Virgin Mary. On the lower part of the vault, there is a Latin inscription: "Egreditur virga de radice Jesse et flos de radice ejus ascendet et requiescet super eum Spiritus Domini", meaning: "A shoot shall sprout from the stump of Jesse and from his roots a bud shall blossom". "The Spirit of God shall be with it".

The Windows: The translucent panels of stained glass set in lead were made by Auguste Labouret. They contain symbols of the virtues of Saint Joseph:

Humility, symbolized by a *violet plant*
Chastety, symbolized by a *lily*
Faith, symbolized by a *anchor*

The chapel decoration was executed by the "Compagnie Canadienne de Carrelages". The entrance is bordered by two columns of antique red marble with Indiana stone capitals depicting the work of Saint Joseph as a carpenter.

E. THE CHAPEL OF SAINT BENEDICT:

This chapel was donated to the Shrine by Bishop Alfred Langlois of Valleyfield on behalf of his diocese. It was completed in the year 1947 and dedicated to Saint Benedict, patron saint of the diocese.

The Floor: The pavement is of gray marble with red, black and yellow marble ornaments.

The Altar:

The Altar-step: It is similar to the floor, but the riser is of red marble decorated with mosaic motifs.

The Altar-Table: Black granite with a band of triangles.

The Altar-Support: It is of white Carrara marble with gold mosaics and a Latin inscription: "Ora et labora", meaning: "Pray and Work", the motto of the Benedictine monks.

The Retable: It is of yellow Sienna marble.

The Statue: Standing on a pedestal of Carrara marble, this tulip-wood statue was carved by H. Angers of Quebec and polychromed at the Quebec studio of the Good Shepherd Sisters, under the direction of Sister St-Amédée. It portrays Saint Benedict with a wooden crosier, the symbol of the Abbot's office in one hand, and the book of the Benedictine rule in the other.

The Walls: They are covered with whitish marble called "Botticino", between the panels, there is a streak of gold mosaic. The cornice has been carved and ornamented with a rope motif. The panels on both sides of the statue bear the arms of Bishop Langlois and of the Valleyfield Diocese.

The Vault: It is a soft blue mosaic made by Auguste Labouret. The subject is the prayer-book called the Breviary, with the seven canonical hours of the day: Matins, Lauds, Prime, Terce, Sext, None, Vespers and Compline. To recite the office of the Word is one of the essential tasks of the Benedictine life.

The Windows: The panels are of thin stained glass set in lead by the Auguste Labouret workshop and they symbolically represent the virtues of Saint Benedict:

Work, symbolized by a *beehive.*
Contemplation, symbolized by an *eagle.*
Prudence, symbolized by a *burning lamp.*

The marble work was executed by the Henreaux De Querceta firm of Italy; the finish work was done by the "Compagnie Canadienne de Carrelages". The two columns at the entrance to the chapel are of yellow Sienna marble; their diameter is 12,5 inches.

F. THE CHAPEL OF SAINT JEAN-BAPTISTE-DE-LASALLE:

The Christian Brothers, many of whom had taught at Sainte-Anne-de-Beaupré, donated the chapel, which was dedicated to their founder, Saint Jean-Baptiste-de-LaSalle in 1945.

The Floor: The pavement is of gray marble, but it is decorated with many strips of varied colors.

The Altar:

The Altar Step: It is mostly of red marble with glints of peach pink.

The Altar-Table: It is of grazed black Belgian "petit granit".

The Altar-Support: It is made of red marble like the four pillars and the two pilasters flanking the mosaic which represents the Christian Brothers' coat of arms.

The Pedestal and the Statue: The white marble statue which stands on a pedestal of red marble was provided by the Christian Brothers; they themselves had the pedestal made in Italy by Italian sculptor Ciochetti. The pedestal bears the Latin inscription: "Sinite parvulos venire ad me", meaning: "Let the children come to me".

The Walls: They are coated with gray marble, with a star carved in the upper part of the panels. There are two Latin inscriptions: "Venite filii, audite me", meaning: "Come my sons, listen to me" and the continuation of the former inscription: "Timorem Domini docebo vos", "I will teach you to stand in awe of the Lord". The cornice carved in white marble is decorated with a cross motif.

The Vault: It is a light blue mosaic made by Auguste Labouret. At the top, there is a huge star similar to the one found on the coat of arms of Saint Jean-Baptiste-de-LaSalle, and accompanied by two Angels with spread-out wings. A Latin inscription explains the star: "Et qui ad justitiam erudiunt multos quasi stellae ad perpetuas aeternitates", "Those who lead the crowds on the right way, will shine like stars for all eternity". Small stars surround the large one. There are also, in the lower part of the vault, pictorial references to the main ideas of the Christian Brothers' spirituality: love of the crucifix, Adoration of the Blessed Sacrament, Charity, the Bible, Fasting, the Holy Communion.

The Stained Glass Windows: The panels were made of thin glass set in lead by Auguste Labouret and represent symbols of the virtues that highlighted the life of Saint Jean-Baptiste-de-LaSalle:

Charity, symbolized by a *few buns.*
Love of God, symbolized by a *burning torch.*
Patience, symbolized by *thorns.*

The work was executed by the "Compagnie Canadienne de Carrelages" of Montreal. The two columns at the entrance are of antique red marble.

G. THE CHAPEL OF SAINT JOACHIM:

This chapel dedicated to Saint Joachim, Saint Ann's spouse, was donated to the Shrine by the Diocese of Saint-Jean of Quebec, at the request of Bishop Anastase Forget. This chapel, contrary to the others, was not designed by Audet, but by assistant architect Beaulé.

The Floor: The pavement is of green marble from Tennessee, with decorations of black marble, of red Levato Marble and of yellow Verona marble.

The Altar:

The Altar-Step: It is of gray marble from Tennessee.

The Altar-Table: It is made of two layers of marble: one slab, antique red and the other, black with gold streaks.

The Altar-Support: Placed between two columns of yellow Verona marble, the large panel of antique red marble bears the Latin inscription: "O Joachim, sanctae conjux Annae, pater almae Virginis", "O Joachim, Saint Ann's spouse and father of the Blessed Virgin".

The Pedestal and the Statue: The pedestal of yellow Verona marble is decorated with a mosaic picturing two doves. The statue was made in Italy of marble of different colors.

The Wall: It is coated with Travertine panels held in place by rectangular studs. At first, only the arms of the St-Jean diocese and those of Bishop Anastase Forget had been put on the wall. But, later, Bishop Coderre had his own arms pictured there too. The radiator hood is an aluminium grille. The sculptured cornice is of "logan cream" stone.

The Vault: It is a mosaic designed and executed by Walter del Mistro: ornamental strips of vivid colors and two scenes from Saint Ann's life on both sides of the altar: the wedding of Saint Ann and Joachim and the meeting at the Golden Gate.

The Windows: They are paneled with thin stained glass set in lead by Auguste Labouret. The symbols illustrate Saint Joachim's virtues:

The *hand* and *gold coins* symbolize *charity*.
The *somptuously ornate temple* symbolizes *religion*.
The *hawthorn branch* and *flowers* symbolize *hope*.

Yellow Vienna marble was used for the entrance columns. The chapel was produced by Terrazzo, Mosaics and Tiles Inc. of Quebec.

H. THE CHAPEL OF SAINT JOHN, THE BAPTIZER:

In 1946, Mr. Charrier of Charrier & Dugal Co. donated this chapel dedicated to Saint John, the Baptizer.

The Floor: It is made up of alternate strips of gray Canadian marble and antique red marble.

The Altar:

The Altar-Step: The same red and gray marbles as above are framed in black marble. The red marble riser is adorned with mosaic motifs.

The Altar-Table: It is of ornamented black Alma granite.

The Altar-Support and the Credence: They are made of antique red marble with gray marble pilasters decorated with maple leaves and samaras.

The Triptych: A first triptych was carved in wood by Alphonse Paré; it is now exposed in the Museum. Mr. Charrier wanted a marble sculpture. So, the St-Henreaux firm commissioned sculptor Cova to produce the polychrome marble triptych that is now in the chapel. In the center, the Precursor with a yellow marble cloak. Two white marble panels: the baptism of Jesus and the beheading of Saint John, the Baptizer. Saint John's head is carried on a tray by Salome.

The Walls: Panels of gray marble from Missisquoi separated by strips of antique red marble cover the walls. On the upper part of the panels, there are carved maple leaves. In the whitish stone cornice, Maurice Lord has sculptured more maple leaves.

The Vault: It is another of Auguste Labouret's mosaics, which represents the Angel of the Canadian fatherland on a background of maple leaves.

The Windows: Paneled with thin stained glass set in lead by Auguste Labouret, they picture symbols of the virtues of Saint John, the Baptizer:

The *wings* symbolize the *gift of prophecy.*
The *thorns, penance.*
The *oak, fortitude.*

The finish work on the chapel was done by the "Compagnie Canadienne de Carrelages". The columns at the entrance of the chapel are of red Alpine marble.

I. THE CHAPEL OF THE BLESSED SACRAMENT:

This chapel, like that of Our Lady of Perpetual Help, is located at the intersection of the ambulatory proper and the transept. It has, therefore, two openings on the ambulatory and is surrounded with arcades, ornamental sculptures and columns. The columns on the ambulatory side are of antique red marble and those on the transept side are of red stalagmatic marble.

This chapel was donated by the Montreal archdiocese and its two suffragan dioceses of Joliette and St-Hyacinthe; the other two suffragan dioceses already had their own chapels.

The Blessed Sacrament Reservation is kept in this chapel on certain occasions; it has then been arranged in view of this service. Contrary to the chapel of the Virgin which makes a pair with it, this chapel has its altar placed in the middle of the floor and specially equipped with two tables and a tabernacle.

The Floor: The pavement is of red marble and gray Bordiglio marble with numerous ornamental motifs.

The Altar:

The Altar-Step: On both sides, it is of the same two kinds of marble as the floor.

The Altar-Tables: They are of black "petit granit".

The Altar-Support: It is of white marble with superb low-relief sculptures enhanced by graceful embroideries of gilt mosaic. On the front of the support facing the wall, there is a representation of the Pascal Lamb; on the front facing the transept, four pretty birds are represented picking grapes.

The Tabernacle: The tabernacle that was installed in the chapel had been made for the main altar. Designed by Louis-N. Audet, it is of steel insulated with asbestos and lined inside with cedar from Brazil. The decorations comprising four adoring Angels are gold plated.

The Walls: Wide arches of Indiana stone separate panels of mosaic with a golden background made by Auguste Labouret. Two vast scenes stand out: The Eucharistic Heart of Jesus and, facing the ambulatory, the Disciples of Emmaus.

The Vault: It also is covered with a mosaic decoration by Auguste Labouret. In the middle of the vault, there shines a large golden sun and all around the vault, there runs a long festoon of wheat heads and grape clusters. The words of the Consecration appear in bold letters: "Take this and eat, this is my body", "Take this and drink, this is my blood". The vault pendentives bear four symbols: a crown of thorns, a globe, a heart pierced with a lance, a chalice and host.

The Windows: Two stained glass windows pierce the cupola; they were made of thick, concrete-set glass by Auguste Labouret. One pictures a chalice, the other, a monstrance.

The Balustrades: They were made of bronze by Albert Gilles of Cowansville. Twenty copper panels with silver represent Eucharistic symbols:

On the Ambulatory Side:
A chalice and a host
A heart
The Holy Spirit and a host
A pelican
A wheat head and a cluster of grapes

On the Transept Side:
Birds drinking from the cup of life
A deer and a fountain
The Eucharistic Heart
The Mystical Lamb
Fishes

The marble pieces were cut by the S. Henreaux firm of Querceta, Italy and they were laid by the "Compagnie Canadienne de Carrelages" of Montreal.

J. THE CHAPEL OF SAINT GERARD:

It was donated to the Shrine in 1946 by Mrs. Elizabeth B. Crane and Mr. George W. Burkitt.

The Floor: The altar is in the front part of the chapel, because, in the back, there are stairs leading to the crypt.

The Altar:

The Altar-Step: It is of green marble dressed with black marble pieces.

The Altar-Table: It is of black granite.

The Altar-Support: Four pilasters of green Saint-Denis marble separate panels of green cipolin marble. In the middle, there is a panel of chased copper, plated with silver, a work by Albert Gilles of Cowansville. It represents Saint Gerard Majella receiving buns from the Infant-Jesus. This scene refers to a episode in Saint Gerard's life as a child.

The Retable: It is of green cipolin marble. A Latin inscription runs on both sides of the small niche: "Absconditi haec sapientibus et prudentibus et revelasti ae parvulis", which means: "You have concealed these things from wise and prudent men, but you have revealed them to young children". In the niche, there is a statue of Saint Gerard Majella created by S. Henreaux Co. of Querceta, Italy.

The Vault: It is covered with a cream-toned mosaic portraying Saint Gerard Majella surrounded by four Angels. The Latin inscription, "Et erunt sicut angeli Dei" means, "They will be like God's Angels".

The Windows: They are decorated with thin, lead-set stained glass made by Auguste Labouret in his Paris workshop. The following virtues of Saint Gerard Majella's are represented:

A *burning bush* symbolizes *love of God.*
A *ladder* symbolizes *perfection.*
A *closed book* symbolizes *wisdom.*

The Gates: A wrought iron work heightened with bronze by the Lebrun Brothers of Three-Rivers after the design produced by co-architect Maxime Roisin during his stay in Canada.

The Marble, cut by the S. Henreaux firm of Querceta, was laid by the "Compagnie Canadienne de Carrelages". The entrance columns are of forest-green marble.

A Closing Word about the Radiating Chapels:

There is a great variety of the finish of the chapels, but Louis-N. Audet managed to safeguard the *unity* of the whole by maintaining in the decoration of each chapel an *element of stability,* namely: *the entrance,* which always follows *the same pattern:* two marble columns support a wide arch and the same black marble is used for the bases of all the columns and the baseboards of all the chapels. It is also worth noting that, in the floor of each chapel, there is always a decorative strip which harmonizes the particular tone of the floor with the black marble of the baseboards and of the bases of the columns. The decoration work on the entrance to the chapels was done by Martineau Co., which shaped the marble columns and had the capitals carved in Indiana stone. The above description of the chapels was taken from documents prepared by Louis-N. Audet and kept in the Shrine's archives. (ASA, B-10a, b.8/doc. 15 651 and ASA, B-10a, b.14/doc. 17 745 to 17 767)

D. THE SACRISTY:

Between the chapels of Saint Benedict and of Saint Jean-Baptiste-de-LaSalle, there is an arch similar to those at the entrance of the chapels. This arch rests on two columns of forest-green marble and frames another arch resting on two columns of antique red marble. It is the entrance to the sacristy of the Basilica.

The Doors of the sacristy:

Made of oak, they were decorated by sculptor Vallières of St-Romuald. The sculptures represent the four cardinal virtues:

Justice: A symbolic figure holds an escutcheon bearing the image of a bird and a Latin inscription, "Justus ut palma florebit", meaning, "The just shall blossom like a palm branch". Justice here means more than respect for another's property or rights; according to the Bible, it stands for loyalty and perfection.

Fortitude: A warrior holds a shield with the picture of a lion on it. One can also read on the shield the Latin words, "Collidam in te equium (sic) et equitem", which means, "With you, I have wrought the horse, together with the horseman". (Jer. 5, 21, BDJ, p. 1,221)

Prudence: A human figure holds an escutcheon with the image of a snake and the Latin inscription, "Estote prudentes sicut serpentes", meaning, "Be as prudent as snakes".

Temperance: It means here simplicity and humility. A symbolic figure holds an escutcheon decked with the picture of a dove and the Latin words, "Simplices sicut columbae", which mean, "As humble as doves".

The vestibule serving as a passage between the sacristy and the lower as well as the upper church, is decorated with a Holy Spirit emblem in mosaic and is finished with Manitoba stone, the kind that the architects had first intended to use for the interior coating of the entire Basilica. A spiral staircase leads to the crypt or lower church. It is not accessible to visitors.

The *sacristy* proper is a vast hall which serves as the vestry of the Basilica. The numerous sacred vessels and vestments used during divine service are kept there. The sacristy was finished with oak by the carpenters of the Basilica and especially by Réal Cayouette, who made the wardrobes. The wooden sculptures on the niches were made by Wilfrid Richard: small statues of the Sacred Heart, the Virgin Mary, Saint Ann and Saint Alphonsus. Wilfrid Richard has also decorated the wooden altar and the baptismal font in the sacristy. And in the reredos of the baptismal font, he carved the Baptism of Jesus in low relief. Above the door leading to the parlors, there is a very beautiful copy of Raphael's tableau, the *"Transfiguration of Christ"*.

E. THE INSIGNIA OF THE BASILICA:

At the end of the ambulatory, near Saint Gerard's chapel, two ornaments have been placed well in view in the corner of the transept: they are the insignia of the Basilica. The word, "Basilica" comes from the Greek word "basileus", which means "king". It is a title granted by the Roman Catholic Pontiff to certain churches, because of their antiquity or of any other feature that highlights the importance of these churches in the Catholic world. The title of Basilica was bestowed upon the first Shrine of Sainte-Anne-de-Beaupré by Leo XIII, on May 7, 1887. There are two kinds of Basilicas: the major Basilicas which have to be in Rome and the minor ones which may be anywhere in the world. Sainte-Anne-de-Beaupré's is therefore a minor Basilica, having its own insignia or arms represented on a shield. The two distinctive elements are the *procession banner* and the *pilgrimage bells.* Old photographs dating back to the beginning of the century, show that the insignia of the Basilica used to be carried along during solemn processions in honor of Saint Ann. The insignia bear, by mistakes, the pontifical emblem reserved to major Basilicas. Therefore, according to a decision by Monsignor Dante, master of ceremonies at Saint-Peter's in Rome, the insignia of Saint Ann's Basilica may not be used during processions (ASA, P-13a, b.1/doc. 2,678 and PA-11, b.1/doc.2,629) The keys of Saint Peter would have to be replaced by another symbol. The arms of the Basilica can be described as follows in heraldic lingo:

"Azure, a Latin cross silver with a lance and a reed crosswise thereon, set upon a mountain with three summits alike, which is of the Redemptorists; in the chief, a crown silver and sable with a Saint Ann holding the Virgin on her right arm gold; the shield is bordered on the sides by two boughs with lower ends joined, of oak leaves gold dexter (on the right) and of maple leaves of the same sinister (on the left). Above the shield, a pontifical flag with bands gold and gules alternatively". (ABSA, vol. 85, p. 288)

9. THE CHOIR LOFT

(Before going down to the chapel by the stairs near the Holy Family altar, let us go toward the center of the church near the communion rail and have a look at the choir loft.)

The choir loft is the place reserved to the church chorus and the organ. Father Nadeau briefly described the original feature of the choir loft:

"At Sainte-Anne-de-Beaupré, one is not, as it were, crushed under a deep gallery that would extend over two spans of columns and destroy the perspective of a church. Here, the choir loft is confined to the space above the vestibule". (ABSA, 1923, p. 259)

When the interior of the Basilica was finished, a depressed arch, spanning the whole width of the nave, was made to support the choir loft. Above all, two elements of the choir loft call for attention: the rose window and the organ.

A. THE ROSE WINDOW:

The rose window or "great rose" lets in the afternoon light; it is made up of 37 panels of thick stained glass set in concrete and its beauty is heightened by nine parallel windows placed under it like a luminous pedestal.

The rose has a diameter of 23 feet. The stone of the rose was not quarried at Saint-Sébastien of Beauce like that of the rest of the Basilica. It is G. Plamondon of Saint-Samuel who carved the one-foot thick blocks out of granite from Stanstead. He completed this work in 1928 and died in May 1941.

According to his own testimony, this work had been the most beautiful he had ever done in all his life.

Auguste Labouret made the stained glass panels after his own technique of thick, chipped glass set in concrete. In the middle, stands Saint Ann with the Virgin and the Infant Jesus, a typical representation in Saint Ann's hagiography. It is often called "The Saint Ann Trinity". All around, there are invocations from the litanies to the Blessed Virgin. In the nine vertical windows below the rose, burning lamps represent the sensible virgins of the parable and the non-burning ones symbolize the foolish virgins.

B. THE ORGAN:

The organ of the Basilica is a product of Casavant & Brothers of Saint-Hyacinthe. The console occupies the middle of the choir loft steps and the pipes are hidden in the recesses on both sides. On December 16, 1945, Monsignor Georges-Léon Pelletier, auxiliary Bishop of Quebec blessed the organ. The organ is equipped with 39 stops as follows: 10 at the grand organ, 12 at the swell-organ, 10 at the choir-organ, 7 at the swell-pedal. There are also 20 accompaniment registers. The pipes number 2,700.

10. THE CHAPEL OF THE IMMACULATE CONCEPTION

The Lower Church is called "The Chapel of the Immaculate Conception", as it has been dedicated to Mary, the daughter of Saint Ann. The statue of the Virgin Mary seen above the main-altar, stands out against the background of organ pipes; this arrangement symbolizes the perfect harmony that prevails in the heart of the Virgin Mary, more beautiful than all the symphony of creation. Her features express her inward feelings and respect for God. She is the Meditative Virgin. As for the all blue decoration, it gives an atmosphere completely marian to this chapel.

Almost as spacious as the nave of the Basilica, it is used for

East

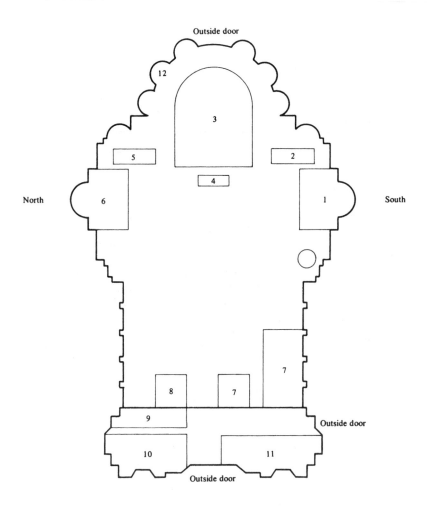

Outside door

North

South

West

large pilgrimage gatherings and to promote the coming together of the parochial community. So, when large groups need a place to meet or talk, the Chapel of the Immaculate Conception gives them the space required for this purpose.

The blue mosaic vault illustrates a starry night sprinkled with stars. This work was carried out by Del Mistro in 1987.

The wall frescoes are the work of the painter Frédéric Doyon.

In the sanctuary, two paintings of Saint Ann and her Daughter are shown to convey the bond which exists between Mary and her mother.

On the south side, The Magi, guided by the star, arrive at the manger. At the center of this painting, we see the hands of God which preside over the destinies of mankind, by offering the Redeemer. The Magi's star and the cross spring up from his hands. "In addition to representing God, says Frederic, these hands replace the "self-portrait" associated with the Renaissance's painters". Jesus, sitting on his mother's knees , is not afraid of these strangers who are the Wise Men. Rather, they arouse his curiosity; he looks at them somewhat in amusing wonder. As for his mother, she seems a little embarrassed in front of these strange personages unknown to her. Joseph, then, reacts like the family guardian: he puts his hand on his wife's knee to reassure her. An unprecedented gesture in iconography.

The Wise Men's group represents the theological virtues and is in direct contrast with the one located on the north side by the exuberant personages and opulence of the material. Here, Mary, on her knees, holding a lily in her hand, is presented at the Temple by her mother, Ann, who puts her hand on her daughter's head as a sign of offering. Behind her, stands Elizabeth, mother of John the Baptist and Joachim. In front, the priests and the levite. One of the High Priests welcomes little Mary, while another carries the Book of the Law and the levite, on his knees, holds in his hand the censer.

In the nave, on the north side, appears a triptych. This fresco in three paintings shows Joachim's family in prayer. It illustrates the development of the marian cult based on the teaching of the Fathers of the Church. The center painting portrays Mary sitting on the knees of her father Joachim. Ann, standing, holds her hand on her daughter's head, while the dove, symbol of the Holy Ghost, flies over the three personages. The painting on the left illustrates the Greek Fathers Jean of Damas and Cyrille of Alexandria. Jean of Damas wrote considerably about the Virgin Mary, while Cyrille was the main supporter of the divine motherhood at the Council of Ephesus around 431. The other painting shows Ignace of Antioche and Irénée of Lyon, both martyrs during the first centuries of the Church. The first, a disciple of the Apostle Jean, is witness of Mary, Mother of the Church, while Irénée establishes a parallel between Eve and Mary.

Another triptych was planned to appear on the south side wall. You would have seen, in the central panel, Mary and Joseph in worship before the Divine Son, and, in the lateral panels, four Fathers from the Western Church, who have also worked considerably towards the development of the cult to Mary. But the death of the painter Frédéric has deferred this project till later.

One hundred and seventy-eight mosaics inlays decorate the pillars in the Chapel of the Immaculate Conception. In their own way, they sing the Hymn of the three children as reported in the Book of Daniel. All the creatures praise Mary: the flowers, the birds, the butterflies, the precious stones, the amanitas, meaning the Caesar's mushrooms. These mosaics were carried out by the Spilimbergo School of Mosaic, near Venise, and are part of the long tradition of byzantine mosaic.

1. THE CHAPEL OF THE BLESSED SACRAMENT

On the transept south side you will find the *Chapel of the Blessed Sacrament*. This chapel was set up to facilitate meditation for those small groups who would prefer more discreet celebrations.

Every day of the year, at 7:10 a.m., a mass is celebrated in this chapel. This Eucharist is broadcasted on the local community TV channel for the benefit of those persons in the region who can't easily go to church.

2. THE CHAPEL OF THE PIETA

In this meditation chapel stands a copy of Michelangelo's Pieta. For more information on this subject, we refer you to the book entitled "The Pieta" by Father Laurent Proulx.

3. THE RELIQUARY OF FATHER ALFRED PAMPALON

Born in 1867 in Lévis, P.Q., although in poor health, the young Alfred Pampalon joined the Redemptorist Order in 1886. At that time, he had to go to Belgium for his novitiate and theological studies. In 1895, he came back sapped by tuberculosis; nevertheless, he spent the last year of his life actively participating in the Basilica's pastoral. His concern and compassion for people suffering from alcoholism was commendable. He died the following year, on September 30, 1896. His personal papers revealed the extremely high quality of his spiritual life; most of all, the courage he showed during his long illness called for admiration.

His remains are preserved in a reliquary placed in a tomb made of black granite. These remains were treated by a doctor and then wrapped in silk. On his tomb, the coat-of-arms of the Redemptorist Congregation can be seen: JS and MA (Jesus-Maria), the spear and sponge which remind us of the Calvary scene and the triangle in God's eye which represents the Unity in the Trinity.

Father Pampalon has been proclaimed Venerable, following the decree on the heroical quality of virtues. More and more pilgrims invoke him, specially those who suffer from drug dependencies or alcoholism.

4. THE COUNSELING OFFICES

Two counseling offices are available to the visitors who wish to consult a priest or another person designated by the guardians responsible for the sanctuary. One of these offices is located in the Chapel of the Immaculate Conception, at the foot of the stairs and the other one is located in the vestibule. If you need to meet and talk to someone about personal problems, that is where you should go.

5. THE ORGAN IN THE CHAPEL OF THE IMMACULATE CONCEPTION

The organ we see in the sanctuary were built in 1986 by Guilbault and Therien.

6. SAINT ANN'S AIDES QUARTERS

Saint Ann's Aides quarters are located under the front steps of the Basilica and are used as a rallying location for their activities. It is also where numerous stretchers and wheelchairs for the sick and handicapped pilgrims are stored.

11. THE MEMORIAL CHAPEL:

(The visit of the Basilica is now over. We suggest that you go out through the door of the north transept of the crypt and proceed to the memorial chapel often called the "old church". The diagram indicates the way.

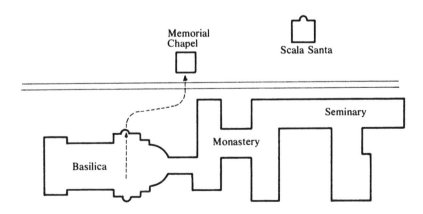

Once out of the Basilica, you go across the square to the exit near the Monastery. Then, you cross the street, which in old days was the King's Road, and please stop in front of the memorial chapel).

1. SAINT ANN'S FOUNTAIN AND ITS STORY:

In front of the memorial chapel, stands *Saint Ann's fountain,* where visitors come to drink *"Saint Ann's water"*. Here is what Father N.-A. Leclerc wrote in 1875:

"A modest fountain, but which attracts the attention of all pilgrims. They approach it with respect and confidence. According to the testimony of a great number of sick people, this water has worked innumerable prodigious cures" (ABSA, 1875, vol. 2, p. 244)

There is no precise document permitting to pinpoint the date when the whole thing began. But, in 1873, when the "Annals of Good Saint Ann" began to be printed, the existence of the fountain was a known fact. There are references to "the water of the mountain where people go to drink". As a matter of fact, the water of the fountain springs naturally from the hillside. It is protected by a small structure topped with a statue of Saint Ann, which can be seen along the path leading to the Scala Santa.

The first work on the fountain was done in 1876, when it was fitted with a 144 cubic-foot tank and pipes carrying the water to a place in front of the old church. There, an octagonal basin of cut stone was built with a statue of Saint Ann in the center.

But, in 1926, the King's road had to be widened, so the fountain in front of the memorial church was rearranged accordingly with new steps and all, so that after three years, everything was ready for the 1929 pilgrimage season. Gaudiose Plamondon of Saint-Samuel of Stanstead is responsible for the final arrangement of the fountain, namely a platform with steps leading to the memorial chapel and stairs on both sides with converging paths leading to the Scala Santa and to the Stations of the Cross. In the center of the fountain, there is a granite pillar of a maximum diameter of 30 inches, topped by a statue of

Saint Ann. The statue is made of wood with a gilt weatherproof coating. It is a sculpture by Louis Jobin, whose signature can be seen on the base a little in the back. The water of the fountain is now carried by pipes to the church store, where it can be had even in winter.

2. THE MEMORIAL CHAPEL:

This chapel often called the "old church" is not the church that was used for pilgrimages for two centuries at Sainte-Anne-de-Beaupré. It is a chapel that has been built with the remaining materials of the old church, on the site where the transept of the old church was.

THE OLD CHURCH

Built in 1676, it had been renovated, enlarged and embellished many times before it was demolished in 1877 to make room for the memorial chapel. At that time, it was 100 feet long, 30 feet wide and 40 feet high. The floor plan was a Latin cross with the top of the upright rounded. The exterior and interior walls were whitewashed. The facade, being on the west side, faced the old cemetery and had only one large door. Above the door there was a bull's-eye over which there was a small niche where stood the little statue of Saint Ann, which is now exposed in the Museum. In the wall along Royal Avenue, a side-door had been cut at an unknown time. The roof, which had at first been covered with slates, was then covered with cedar shingles. A cross, surmounted by a Gallic rooster, topped the steeple. This steeple had first been built by carpenters Robert Leclaire and Jean Marchand in 1693 after Claude Baillif's drawings; it had then been replaced by a smaller and lighter steeple inspired by

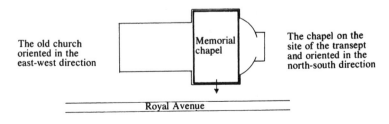

The old church oriented in the east-west direction

Memorial chapel

The chapel on the site of the transept and oriented in the north-south direction

Royal Avenue

the same plans. It is this latter steeple which has been installed on the memorial chapel.

The interior wall finish was nothing but whitewash, but the ceiling had been painted azure and spangled with golden stars. In the sanctuary, there were Corinthian style panels, cornices and pillars, with white and gold decorations. Wooden chandeliers hung from the vault. Once a year, they used to be lowered to be furnished with tallow candles on the occasion of the Christmas midnight Mass.

When Father Jean-Baptiste Blouin thought of building the new church along the King's road in 1871, the old church was falling into ruins. The north wall was about to collapse because of water infiltration from the hillside; many sections of the roof also had rotten. In spite of opposition from many well known personalities, Monsignor Gauvreau, then parish priest at Sainte-Anne, had his way and he built, on the site of the old church transept, "a chapel for processions and pilgrimages". (ASA, PA-16, doc. 4,411, passim)

THE COMMEMORATIVE CHAPEL OR MEMORIAL CHURCH

This chapel was open for worship on October 2, 1878; Monsignor Gauvreau blessed it, leaving the interior to be finished by his successors, the Redemptorist Fathers.

The finish work on the interior of the chapel was completed in 1881, under the supervision of Father Tielen, then religious superior at Sainte-Anne-de-Beaupré.

Between October 1965 and April 1966, at the Redemptorists' request, the "Arts Religieux Appliqués" renovated the memorial chapel. Mario Mauro, assisted by Carlo Marzaro, executed the work after studying old photographs of the chapel. The vault was restored as before and the gilt work on the main altar and the pulpit was retouched. As for the side altars, they were restored, but they were transferred to the Museum, on the first floor. A wood sculptor by the name of Trudelle renewed the missing ornaments. He produced 200 ornamental pieces to complete here and there the cornices, the capitals, the columns, the retables and the picture frames. The paintings now on the walls of the memorial chapel are *copies* of the originals, which have been transferred to the first floor of the Museum. The original paintings would have deteriorated during winter because the chapel is not heated.

The memorial chapel is 45 feet long and 35 feet wide.

The Exterior of the Chapel

The stones of the old chapel were used in the new walls. The door and the openings in the facade, which is now on the south side, contrary to the old church which faced the west, are also authentic pieces from the old church built in 1662. What is new is the *slant of the roof* which is not so steep as in the old church. The steeple is the one described above and it contains the bell named "Marie-Anne", dating back to 1863.

The Interior

The Vault: The vault of the old church had been completed between 1790 and 1792 and repainted and regilt between 1819 and 1822. The existing vault of the memorial chapel has been adorned with part of the original decoration. (ABSA, vol. 34, p. 360 and ABSA, vol. 35, p. 37)

The Altar-Piece: "The altar-piece of Sainte-Anne-de-Beaupré was carved about the year 1700 by sculptors of the school of Saint-Joachim. The present memorial chapel preserves what has been left of it, namely 4 columns, one tabernacle and two statues representing Saint Magdalen and Saint John... The columns festooned with sculptured flowers at the base, appear in harmony with the Ange-Gardien work" (Jean Trudelle, D.B. D.C., vol. 2, p. 394)

The Main-Altar:

It stands out against the altar-piece. The tabernacle is in the center. "It has few decorations in relief, but its architecture is farfetched, presenting different types of cornices, gables, cupolas, balusters ... as if the idea were to give an example of all the

The old church of Sainte-Anne-de-Beaupré

Built in 1676, it was rebuilt, except for the facade, between 1689 and 1695 after Claude Baillif's drawings; it was partially rebuilt again in 1787-1788. The steeple, made in 1696 by carpenters Robert Leclaire and Jean Marchand after Baillif's drawings, was reconstructed in 1788 according to the same plans; it is this latter steeple that is now in the memorial chapel.

The above print offered by the "Inventaire des Oeuvres d'Art" was taken from the "Bazar", 1886, num. 8 (7-IX), p. 92

elements that can possibly be used in the architecture of a tabernacle". (Jean Trudelle, loc. cit.)

Traditionally, this tabernacle work has been attributed to Jacques Leblond de Latour. But, according to Trudelle, it was rather a group undertaking, the work, though directed by Leblond de Latour, being executed by pupils of the Saint-Joachim school, namely Denis Mallet, Charles Vézina and Pierre Gabriel LePrévost.

In the following years, modifications were made on the tabernacle. In the beginning of 1759, Father Parent, parish priest, had a retable made to serve as a reliquary for the relics of Saint Ann and of other saints. This retable can now be seen in the chapel but with empty pigeon-holes. Later, in 1773, two statues of Angels from the Batiscan factory were placed where they are now, on the retable, after being regilt by the Ursuline Sisters. In 1823, Father Ranvoyzé, Sainte-Ann's parish priest, had the wooden crucifix and the tall candlesticks painted silver by François-Noël Levasseur.

The Pulpit: It was probably bought by Father Ranvoyzé in 1807. It bears a sculpture portraying Moses with the tables of the Law and attributed also to Thomas Baillargé. It was put back in the old church only in 1894, because it had been used in the first Basilica until a huge pulpit was installed there. The latter was destroyed in the 1922 fire.

12. THE SCALA SANTA OR SACRED STAIR

(We suggest now that you leave the memorial chapel and go to the Scala Santa as indicated in the diagram)

1. HOW THE SCALA SANTA WAS BUILT:

Construction began in 1891; on May 24th, Father Ernest Dubois, C.Ss.R., canonical visitor, solemnly blessed the corner stone. On June 16, 1894, the Scala Santa was blessed and inaugurated by Bishop L. Nazaire Bégin. There was a procession to the new chapel and Monsignor Gauvreau, former parish priest of Sainte-Anne's, delivered an appropriate sermon. At that time,

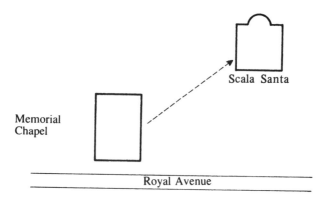

Scala Santa

Memorial
Chapel

Royal Avenue

only the upper part had been fitted up. In 1910, the ground floor was made into a Grotto of the Agony, in memory of Gethsemane. In April 1925, part of the foundations was restored and, on that occasion, the painted parts of the Grotto were retouched. Finally, in 1972, it became necessary to repaint the exterior of the Scala Santa. Now, while workers were removing the old paint with torches, the first floor veranda accidentally caught fire. Fortunately, the fire was quickly put under control. But it was decided to cover the boards with cream-colored aluminum siding. Renovations were completed in 1977, when "Les Arts Appliqués" restored the whole interior of the building. The entire inside surface was lined with insulating materials. A complete new painting job was done. The coloring of the sculptures was retouched and the Grotto of the Agony also was restored.

2. THE SCALA SANTA:

It is a chapel built to shelter the Sacred Stairs. The building is 72 feet long and 36 feet wide. The Sacred Stairs, running from the first floor, consist of 28 steps: underneath them, there is a chapel memorializing the agony of Jesus. The essential function of this building justifies its Italian name of "Scala Santa", which means "Sacred Stairs" and also explains its special architecture. As was said before, the sacred stairs start on the first floor.

By climbing them, you reach the upper chapel. Our description will go from bottom up:

1. On the Ground floor: the Grotto of the Agony

There are three groups of polychrome stucco sculptures after the style of Flemish statues. Like all the statues in the Scala Santa, they were produced in Mathias Zen's workshop at Gand, Belgium. In the center, the Agony of Jesus in the garden; on the right, the Apostles sleeping; on the left, Judas' treacherous kiss. The statues, restored by Arsène Manucci, stand in alcoves decorated with reddish brown titles.

2. On the First Floor: the Sacred Stairs

These stairs represent the steps that the Lord climbed to reach Pilate's court or pretorium. As an act of penance, people climb these stairs on their knees, while reciting the prayers recommended for this exercise of devotion to the Savior's passion. On the panels at the entrance, there are large maps of Palestine and of the city of Jerusalem. Those who do not wish to climb the stairs on their knees may use either of the two side-stairs. Enclosed in each step of the Sacred Stairs, are stones from the places sanctified by the passion of Jesus.

On the walls around the chapel on the first floor, there are paintings by Joseph Soligo. They are identified by the names of the places they represent, places where Jesus lived during his stay on earth. In the back, three sculptured groups: the Calvary, the Pieta and Jesus appearing to Saint Mary Magdalen. Under the altar-table, a carved corpus of Jesus in his tomb. The statues stand on altars made of hard wood and adorned with inscriptions.

3. The Second Floor:

On reaching the top of the Sacred Stairs, one can see three sculptured groups: the Ecce Homo in the center, the flogging of Jesus on the right and Jesus meeting Saint Veronica on the left. The vault of the chapel is decorated with frescoes, where Angels display inscriptions related to the passion of Jesus. On the walls, there are stations of the cross painted on copper by

The pulpit in the old church

It was probably ordered in 1807 by Father Ranvoyzé, Saint-Anne's parish priest. Among sculptures by Thomas Baillargé, there is, in the middle, a medallion representing Moses with the tables of the Law and, in the corners, small Angels heads. (Photo Moderne)

C. Bogaert of Bruges. The images of the way of the cross are enclosed in pictures of the City of Jerusalem where Jesus suffered his passion. Joseph Soligo has completely renovated the iconography of the chapel and the vault which had been created by Brother Ildephonse Lepas, C.Ss.R. In the back of the chapel, stands a statue of the suffering Christ, which had been long venerated in the crypt of the Basilica and was transferred to the Scala Santa in 1977.

The Man of Sorrows is seated on a throne worked up by Octave Morel. The pedestal is four feet high and inlaid with pieces of marble. The upper part is a kind of reredos with an arch and a small canopy. This woodwork was executed in 1915.

13. THE STATIONS OF THE CROSS

(We suggest that you return to the front of the Scala Santa and enter the path of the Stations of the Cross. This walk will lead you to the old cemetery and the Chapel of the Souls.)

A. THE STATIONS OF THE CROSS

The first stations of the cross on the hillside were installed before 1895; they were restored on September 22, 1896 (ASA, Pa-16/doc. 4,413, pp. 237 and 239) They were but wooden crosses set along a path slightly different from the existing one. At the twelfth station, there was a monumental crucifix (The Book of Sermons, 1896 and ASA, Pa-7, b.3/doc. 534)

In 1908, the path was altered and improved. The first Way of the Cross preached on the hillside for pilgrims was the one preached by Father Albert o.f.m.cap. to a group of pilgrims from Limoilou. Little by little, this practice became an essential part in the pilgrimage program and the thought of stations with life-size personages became more and more imperative.

The work was commissioned to a French firm, the "Union Internationale Artistique", registered at Vaucouleurs, France. The first group to be ordered was the twelfth station, namely the Calvary. It was delivered on July 18, 1913. The last station was installed 32 years later, in 1945. A detailed history of each

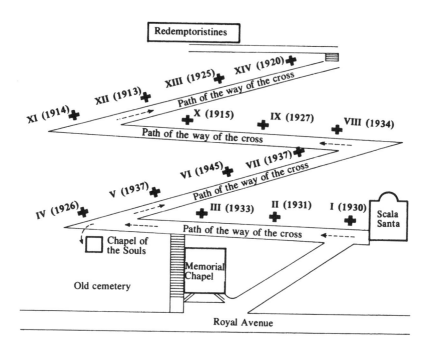

Redemptoristines

XIV (1920)

XIII (1925)

XII (1913)

Path of the way of the cross

XI (1914)

X (1915)

IX (1927)

VIII (1934)

Path of the way of the cross

VII (1937)

VI (1945)

Path of the way of the cross

V (1937)

IV (1926)

III (1933)

II (1931)

I (1930)

Scala Santa

Path of the way of the cross

Chapel of the Souls

Memorial Chapel

Old cemetery

Royal Avenue

group would be too long. Suffice it to say that, during the two World Wars, the foundries were requisitioned and the work on the stations of the Cross was seriouly impaired.

The "Union Internationale des Artistes" of Vaucouleurs was set up towards the end of the nineteenth century, by *Martin Pierson.* It first undertook stone work, then moved to cast iron, to moulding, to bronze work. Under the guidance of the so-called Pierson dynasty, the company prospered. At the time work began of Saint-Ann's stations of the cross, the manager was *Charles Pierson.* He died in 1923 and his son, *Albert Pierson* succeeded him. The stations of the cross at Sainte-Anne-de-Beaupré are made of bronzed cast iron. Five groups similar to those of Sainte-Anne were produced by the same firm and exposed at Huberdeau, Quebec. (Stations 10, 11, 12, 13 and 14)

The models for each station normally required about a year's work. A great deal of preparatory work was necessary:

1. The Designer's Work:

Two designers worked on the stations of the cross for Sainte-Anne-de-Beaupré. The first was *Constant Menissier*, who died in 1916. "He was a man of great talent and we have never been able to find a man of equal skill" (Albert Pierson, September 1949, ASA, B-11d, b.1/doc. 793) The other designer was *Émile Roy*. "He is the one who created your stations of the cross", said Albert Pierson. He had studied sculpture under Victor Huel for 4 years and then had spent some time at the "Beaux Arts" of Nancy. He was 71 years old when he completed his work for Sainte-Anne-de-Beaupré.

2. From the Drawing board to Casting:

When the design is completed, a clay model must be made. Then, from this model, a mould of baked clay (terra cotta) is made in which the iron is cast. When casting is over, the cast is edged off and bronzed. Sainte-Anne's stations of the cross had to be rebronzed many times since its installation, because cold weather kept damaging the bronze coating. It was last restored in 1976 by Maurice Lord, who sandblasted all the statues and had them covered with several coasts of metal paint as is done for automobiles.

Each group is usually made up of five personages and weighs an average of three tons, not counting the crosses. The stations rest on granite bases with a kneeling step along the path for the use of pilgrims.

B. THE CEMETERY:

The cemetery at the bottom of the hill near the fourth station, is called the "Old Cemetery". The last remains to be buried there date back to about 1930. Around that time, another cemetery had been prepared on the east side of the parish. Today, it spreads on both side of Royal Avenue. But, for almost three hundred years, the dead parishioners' remains were buried in the old cemetery. The "Guidebook of the Quebec Railway, Light

The hillside stations of the cross
"Jesus meets the women of Jerusalem", that is the title of this station as it appears on the hillside, under the open sky, to lead you on your devotional way of the cross. The work of the artists of the "Union Internationale des Artistes" of Vaucouleurs is better appreciated when seen in the natural setting for which it was intended. (Photograph by Alain Lesieur)

and Power Company" of the 30's has the following words about the old cemetery:

> "The cemetery, by all appearances so modest, has nevertheless an interesting history.
>
> Inaugurated in 1670, it contains the remains of all those who have died in the parish since its foundation and of many others who chose to rest near Saint Ann's Shrine. From the inauguration of the cemetery till about 1930, the bodies of 3734 people were buried there, among whom there were 74 Indians. A surprising number indeed, considering the fact that the same number of people would not have enough room just to stand upright on such a restricted area. (ASA, B-9d, b.2/doc. 18 369, p. 57)

It must be said however that some remains had been buried under the first Basilica. After the fire of 1922, all the remains in the vault have been transferred to the new cemetery.

C. THE CHAPEL OF THE SOULS:

What had probably been a winter charnel-house, has become the "Chapel of the Souls". As it appears now, it is but a small chapel sheltering a Calvary, made at Mathias Zen's workshop in Gand, Belgium. The walls are covered with commemorative plaques bearing the names of pilgrims who meant to show their families and every body else their intention of keeping a link with Saint Ann's Shrine even after their death.

14. THE BUILDINGS AROUND THE BASILICA

(Before you cross over to the Museum on the south side for the last part of your visit, we would like to comment briefly on the buildings around the Basilica. The diagram identifies each building with a number.)

1. The Redemptoristine's Convent

The building on top of the hill was constructed in 1905 to welcome the cloistered Redemptoristines. Their founder, Venerable Celesta Crostarosa, who is memorized in a stained glass window in the Basilica, was a disciple of Saint Alphonsus Liguori. Their goal is to imitate by their life Jesus the Redeemer

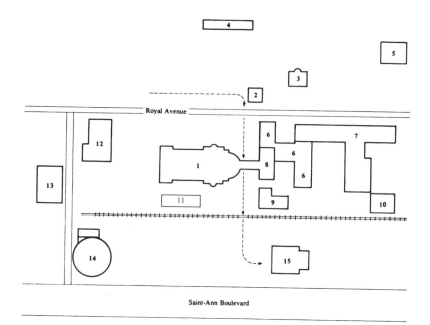

1. Basilica
2. Memorial Chapel
3. Scala Santa
4. Redemptoristine's Convent
5. Franciscan Missionaries of Mary
6. Redemptorist Fathers' Monastery
7. Saint Alphonsus Seminary
8. Church Store
9. Public Rest Rooms
10. Office of The Annals of Saint Anne
11. Information Pavilion
12. Saint Ann's Hospital
13. Basilica Inn
14. Cyclorama
15. Sainte Ann Museum

and to unite by their prayers and their sacrifices for the conversion of sinners. Even while being cloistered, these nuns have always been very close to the spirituality and apostolate of their Redemptorist's brothers.

In 1990, in order to provide more effectively for the health of the sisters and because of the low recruitment, they had to leave Saint Ann's Convent and move to the Sacred Heart General Hospital in Quebec to reside with the Augustine Sisters. Nevertheless, the sisters continue to have a special intention for pilgrims and they offer their prayers and their sacrifices for the Church.

Presently, the Convent is looking for a new vocation and remains under the supervision of maintenance personnel.

2. The Franciscan Missionaries of Mary:

The Franciscan Sisters' convent was first occupied by the Sisters of Charity, who had come from Quebec on October 27, 1871 to establish a convent at Saint-Anne with a school for girls and a boarding house for women on pilgrimage. On September 8, 1897, an agreement was signed between Father René Allard and Sister Marie-Charité de Jésus, representing the Franciscan Missionaries of Mary, to the effect that the latter would relieve the Sisters of Charity by assuming the direction of Saint Ann's hospital. For years, the Franciscan Sisters have lodged women on pilgrimage and offered meals to the pilgrims. Since 1977, they have ceased serving meals. In June 1899, they had ordered the erection of the first chapel that was to be opened to the public and dedicated to the Sacred Heart of Jesus. Construction work was done by contractor Albert Peters.

In December 1924, the Franciscan Sisters had this chapel demolished in order to build a large one. The basement was made into a dining hall. Also, a brick construction was adjoined to the old convent to serve as a convalescence house for sick sisters. Since 1976, the Franciscan Sisters have two dwelling places at Saint-Anne: one is the old convent, the other is a house located in front of the convent, but at the foot of the hill.

3. The Redemptorists' Monastery:

The Redemptorists were called to Sainte-Anne by Bishop Elzéar Alexandre Taschereau, to take charge of the pilgrimage work and of the parish of Sainte-Anne-de-Beaupré. Monsignor Gauvreau, the last parish priest belonging to the diocesan clergy, had forcefully insisted to have a religious congregation take over his functions. The first Redemptorists arrived at Sainte-Anne in the beginning of December 1878; therefore, 1978 was the centenary of their arrival. The first Redemptorists came from Baltimore; they were replaced in 1879 by Fathers from Belgium. In March 1922, the fire that destroyed the Basilica also consumed the Monastery and the Juvenate (seminary). Reconstruction was considered immediately after the fire and Louis-N. Audet, architect of the Basilica drew the plans of the monastery. It was blessed on July 25, 1924. Father Nadeau gave the following description of the Redemptorists' monastery:

"The Redemptorists' monastery has been completed. Its simple lines are reminiscent of the last days of the Middle-Ages. This sturdy granite building with large windows and angle turrets, that break the monotony of the horizontal lines, does not lack originality. With its gables, its non-symetrical but harmonious wings enclosing two courtyards, one of which, that of the garden, is flanked on three sides by comely cloisters in which were cleverly used decorative remnants of the old Basilica, this building is one of the beautiful examples of monastic architecture in our country. Its simple chapel, soberly decorated, spare the eyes the boring sight of commonplace ornaments; it does have some special value". (A.A.S.C., 1925, p. 100)

The remnants of the old Basilica are stone columns from the facade; they now support a sort of covered ambulatory enclosed by sections of the building and opened on a courtyard. About seventy religious men, Fathers and Brothers, occupy the monastery; most of them are assigned to pastoral work at the Shrine, to the Seminary or the Missions. The Monastery of Sainte-Anne-de-Beaupré is also the Provincial house of the French-speaking Redemptorists.

4. Saint Alphonsus Seminary:

This institution was founded in August 1896, under the name of Juvenate of the Redemptorist Fathers. When Father Catulle, C.Ss.R. authorized the opening of a secondary school, the purpose was to instruct the candidates to religious life with the Redemptorists and to form, on the spot, Canadian personnel to replace Belgian groups who were coming from overseas to work in Canada. In 1932, the Juvenate became Saint-Alphonsus Seminary, a house of education affiliated to Laval University and dispensing what was then called the "classical course".

Since 1983, Saint Alphonsus Seminary has been entrusted to a secular corporation. While remaining a catholic school, its main purpose is no longer to receive candidates to the priesthood or religious life. The students, boys and girls, numbering about 180, receive the normal teaching of the first four years of the secondary school.

The blond brick building is remarkable for its roof with Gothic pinnacles; this building takes the place of the one destroyed by fire in March of 1922. The new Juvenate was blessed on May 17, 1923. Behind the facade on the street side, there is a very beautiful chapel with magnificent stained glass windows and decorated with all the boldness of the Gothic tradition.

5. The Church Store:

From immemorial time, there has always existed around the Shrine, a boutique where pious souvenirs of the Shrine and religious articles are sold. The church store is located on the ground floor of the Monastery, behind the apse of the Basilica.

6. The Blessings Office:

While going east, one can see the Blessings Office. From morning till night, visitors and pilgrims come to offer their religious articles or souvenirs to a priest, to be blessed according to the ritual of the Church. Many people take this opportunity to ask for blessings for themselves or to solicit an advice or a prayer to their personal intentions.

7. Food Services and Public Restrooms:

Near the Blessings Office, the pilgrims will find public restrooms, as well as food services and tables where one can take some nourishment.

8. The Office of The Annals of Sainte-Anne-de-Beaupré:

Since 1873, a monthly magazine has been published for the purpose of serving the Church, the family and the Shrine. "Les Annales de la Bonne Sainte-Anne-de-Beaupré", as the magazine was titled when Father N. Leclerc founded it, was first published at Lévis; the Redemptorists bought the organization and transferred it to a place closer to the Shrine. The magazine is published in French and in English. The French edition is titled "La Revue Sainte Anne" and the English edition's title is, "The Annals of Saint Anne de Beaupré". The magazine's office was built in 1938 under the supervision of contractor F.S. Lambert, who was then superintendent of the Basilica. Two sculptures from the old Basilica can be seen inserted on the ground floor of the building; the sculptures of the two gables were made in 1938.

9. The Information Pavilion:

In the Spring of 1999, the guardians of the Shrine inaugurated a new information pavilion to replace the one located on the south side of the Basilica. The purpose of this pavilion is to welcome pilgrims, to give them all the necessary information and to receive mass offerings and subscriptions to the magazine "La Revue Sainte Anne" or "The Annals of Saint Anne de Beaupré".

10. Saint Ann's Hospital:

This elegant granite building was erected in 1930 so as to provide needed medical care and nursing for sick and invalid pilgrims while on a pilgrimage. Over the years, it has been converted into a hospital. With the construction of a regional hospital in Beaupré, the guardians of the Shrine will have to find a new vocation for this building.

11. The Basilica Inn:

Built during the Fall of 1962 and Spring of 1963, the Inn provides lodging for pilgrims, with a preference for those who are handicapped or sick. The three-storey building with brick and stucco walls contains two hundred and twenty beds. The rooms are equipped to accommodate the sick and an elevator service is available at all time. There is also a chapel, a vast lobby, a covered patio and a dining room with cafeteria. The Inn belongs to the pilgrimage organization and is intended for pilgrims.

15. SAINT ANN MUSEUM:[1]

The Historial or Museum of the Basilica, built in 1958 on the occasion of the pilgrimage tercentenary to Sainte-Anne-de-Beaupré, has now been replaced by the Saint Ann Museum.

This project was conceived during the 1980's when the Redemptorists, acknowledging the somewhat antiquated character of the museum and the age of the expositions, considered to renew the contents of the Historial. From 1991 to 1997, a group of people worked hard setting up the exhibit and lay-out of the interior and exterior of the building.

The new Museum opened its doors on June 20, 1997 with a mission of prime importance: offering to pilgrims who come each year to the Shrine of Sainte-Anne-de-Beaupré a supplement to the pilgrimage. Its first vocation: welcoming pilgrims.

Saint Ann Museum: A devotion, a treasure!

Two permanent exhibits share the museum's space. The different objects exhibited are presented in a manner that allows each pilgrim to establish a close link with his personal life experiences.

1. Ground floor exhibit: "All Hails Saint Ann!"

The story of Saint Ann's cult across the world and particularly in North America is introduced. Some spectacular scenes from the wax museum have been renovated and still retain their magic. Various objects from the museum collection and archives of the Basilica are gathered together so that pilgrims can relate their religious practices to the devotion of Saint Ann through their everyday actions. The pilgrims can then explore on their own, the cult's manifestations, discover the many faces of Saint Ann through the continents and centuries.

Here are the main topics:

---

1. This part was written by Julie Simard, Director of the Museum

Zone 1: Saint Ann, Mother of the Virgin Mary and Grandmother of Jesus.

The most important events in the life of Saint Ann represented by wax figure scenes.

Here are the main topics:

Zone 1: Introduction

The current pilgrimage to Sainte-Anne-de-Beaupré is part of an ancient and established tradition and it materializes daily on the grounds and by the contribution of objects.

Zone 2: A millennial and universal cult

The origin of Saint Ann's cult started in the East and spread to the West. Many reproductions of famous paintings of Saint Ann, allow us to note that artists from the East and the West have always been interested in the grandmother of Jesus.

Zone 3: "Good Saint Ann", our model

Saint Ann educates, protects and rescues. Many paintings, supported by numerous testimonies, demonstrate the reasons of this great devotion to Saint Ann.

Zone 4: The North-American Cult

The expansion of Saint Ann's cult in North America and among the Amerindiens is demonstrated by many objects of devotion, The Annals of Saint Anne de Beaupré and the medias. The significant support given by the missionaries, the clergy, the catholic associations and the numerous groups of pilgrims have all contributed to nurture the cult of Good Saint Ann, here at Sainte-Anne-de-Beaupré.

Plan of the ground floor with zones identified

Choice of pictures: wax figure scene "Saint Ann and Saint Joachim at the Golden Gate". Board showing a geographical view of the diffusion to Saint Ann's devotion

2. First floor exhibition: "Pilgrims and pilgrimages at Sainte-Anne-de-Beaupré"

The "treasures" of the collections are shown. These are the

mementoes of more than three hundred years of parochial life and pilgrimage to Sainte-Anne-de-Beaupré. It is evident by the works of art and objects exhibited that the pilgrims' actions have retained their loyalty. The architecture of the two basilicas and events of their construction are well documented and explained.

Zone 2: A pilgrimage, a parish

The beginning of the devotion at Sainte-Anne-de-Beaupré is revealed, first in a parish and rural framework during nearly two centuries. We also learn to know the origin of the votive act which is translated by the representation of ex-votos, tangible signs of acknowledgment for a favour received.

Zone 3: A national pilgrimage

At the turn of the twentieth century, the pilgrimage to Sainte-Anne-de-Beaupré reaches a rapid growth. Its national diffusion gives it, from then on, an outstanding reputation. From this period of growth emerged devotion practices which are associated with the evolution of the pilgrimage site.

Zone 4: A pilgrimage modern and alive

The pilgrimage site had to adapt itself to the realities of modern life and, consequently, a modern and imposing basilica of exceptional beauty, as much from the architectural and artistic point of view, was built.

Plan of the first floor with identified zones

Choice of photographs:
ex-voto of the three Lévis castaways
ex-voto donated by Marquis Tracy
ex-voto from Mr. Roger
ex-voto from Mr. Juing
ex-voto from Madame Robineau of Bécancour
Statue by Louis Jobin (1)
Clay model
Goldsmith's craft
Corpus
Main altar

Sir Prouville Tracy's Ex-Voto

The painting represents Saint Ann and the Virgin with the Eternal Father and the Holy Spirit above them. On the left and right sides respectively, Sir Tracy and his wife dressed as pilgrims. The painting was brought to the Shrine in 1666. (Photo Luke)

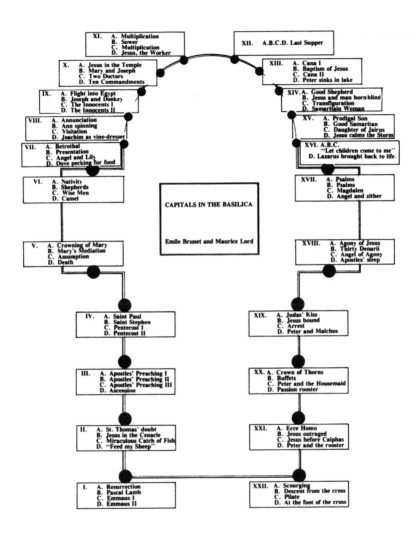

XI.   A. Multiplication
    B. Sower
    C. Multiplication
    D. Jesus, the Worker

XII.   A.B.C.D. Last Supper

X.   A. Jesus in the Temple
    B. Mary and Joseph
    C. Two Doctors
    D. Ten Commandments

XIII.   A. Cana I
    B. Baptism of Jesus
    C. Cana II
    D. Peter sinks in lake

IX.   A. Flight into Egypt
    B. Joseph and Donkey
    C. The Innocents I
    D. The Innocents II

XIV.   A. Good Shepherd
    B. Jesus and man born blind
    C. Transfiguration
    D. Samaritain Woman

VIII.   A. Annunciation
    B. Ann spinning
    C. Visitation
    D. Joachim as vine-dresser

XV.   A. Prodigal Son
    B. Good Samaritan
    C. Daughter of Jairus
    D. Jesus calms the Storm

VII.   A. Betrothal
    B. Presentation
    C. Angel and Lily
    D. Dove pecking for food

XVI.   A.B.C.
    "Let children come to me"
    D. Lazarus brought back to life.

VI.   A. Nativity
    B. Shepherds
    C. Wise Men
    D. Camel

XVII.   A. Psalms
    B. Psalms
    C. Magdalen
    D. Angel and zither

CAPITALS IN THE BASILICA

Emile Brunet and Maurice Lord

V.   A. Crowning of Mary
    B. Mary's Mediation
    C. Assumption
    D. Death

XVIII.   A. Agony of Jesus
    B. Thirty Denarii
    C. Angel of Agony
    D. Apostles' sleep

IV.   A. Saint Paul
    B. Saint Stephen
    C. Pentecost I
    D. Pentecost II

XIX.   A. Judas' Kiss
    B. Jesus bound
    C. Arrest
    D. Peter and Malchus

III.   A. Apostles' Preaching I
    B. Apostles' Preaching II
    C. Apostles' Preaching III
    D. Ascension

XX.   A. Crown of Thorns
    B. Buffets
    C. Peter and the Housemaid
    D. Passion rooster

II.   A. St. Thomas' doubt
    B. Jesus in the Cenacle
    C. Miraculous Catch of Fish
    D. "Feed my Sheep"

XXI.   A. Ecce Homo
    B. Jesus outraged
    C. Jesus before Caiphas
    D. Peter and the rooster

I.   A. Resurrection
    B. Pascal Lamb
    C. Emmaus I
    D. Emmaus II

XXII.   A. Scourging
    B. Descent from the cross
    C. Pilate
    D. At the foot of the cross

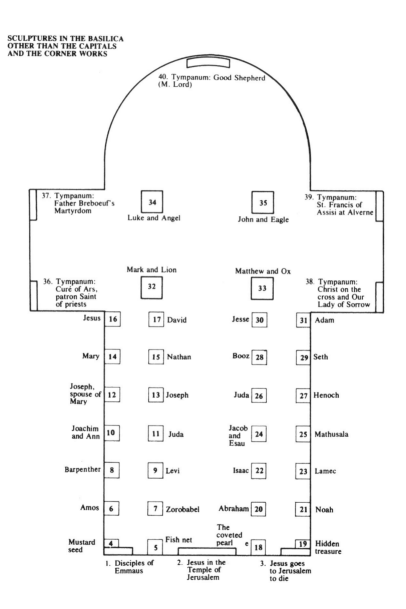

SCULPTURES IN THE BASILICA
OTHER THAN THE CAPITALS
AND THE CORNER WORKS

40. Tympanum: Good Shepherd
(M. Lord)

37. Tympanum:
Father Breboeuf's
Martyrdom

34 Luke and Angel

35 John and Eagle

39. Tympanum:
St. Francis of
Assisi at Alverne

Mark and Lion

36. Tympanum:
Curé of Ars,
patron Saint
of priests

32

Matthew and Ox

33

38. Tympanum:
Christ on the
cross and Our
Lady of Sorrow

Jesus 16

17 David

Jesse 30

31 Adam

Mary 14

15 Nathan

Booz 28

29 Seth

Joseph,
spouse of 12
Mary

13 Joseph

Juda 26

27 Henoch

Joachim
and Ann 10

11 Juda

Jacob
and 24
Esau

25 Mathusala

Barpenther 8

9 Levi

Isaac 22

23 Lamec

Amos 6

7 Zorobabel

Abraham 20

21 Noah

Mustard
seed 4

5 Fish net

The
coveted
pearl e 18

19 Hidden
treasure

1. Disciples of
Emmaus

2. Jesus in the
Temple of
Jerusalem

3. Jesus goes
to Jerusalem
to die

168

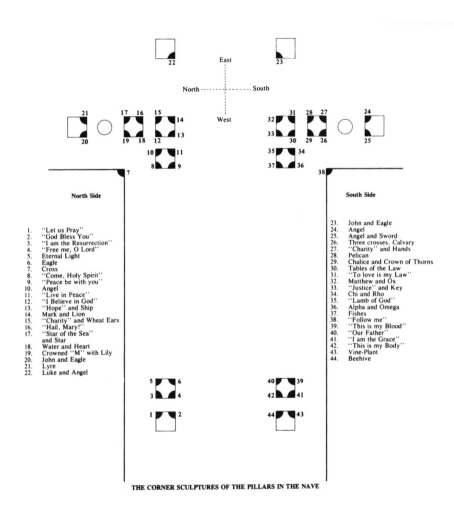

East

North ⌐⌐⌐⌐⌐⌐⌐⌐⌐ South

West

North Side

South Side

1. "Let us Pray"
2. "God Bless You"
3. "I am the Resurrection"
4. "Free me, O Lord"
5. Eternal Light
6. Eagle
7. Cross
8. "Come, Holy Spirit"
9. "Peace be with you"
10. Angel
11. "Live in Peace"
12. "I Believe in God"
13. "Hope" and Ship
14. Mark and Lion
15. "Charity" and Wheat Ears
16. "Hail, Mary!"
17. "Star of the Sea"
    and Star
18. Water and Heart
19. Crowned "M" with Lily
20. John and Eagle
21. Lyre
22. Luke and Angel

23. John and Eagle
24. Angel
25. Angel and Sword
26. Three crosses, Calvary
27. "Charity" and Hands
28. Pelican
29. Chalice and Crown of Thorns
30. Tables of the Law
31. "To love is my Law"
32. Matthew and Ox
33. "Justice" and Key
34. Chi and Rho
35. "Lamb of God"
36. Alpha and Omega
37. Fishes
38. "Follow me"
39. "This is my Blood"
40. "Our Father"
41. "I am the Grace"
42. "This is my Body"
43. Vine-Plant
44. Beehive

THE CORNER SCULPTURES OF THE PILLARS IN THE NAVE

St. Anne's Museum

A dévotion, a treasure

Discover the history of our ancestors through the works of art which describe their devotion to Good Saint Anne.

A visit to the heart of our heritage, from the time of our ancestors of New France to our day, describes this devotion — a treasure.

Schedule Hours

Mid-April to Mid-October
Daily 10:00 am to 5:00 pm

Mid-October to Mid-April
Weekends and Holidays 10:00 am to 5:00 pm

Entrance Fee

Special rates available for families and groups of 20 or more.

For *information and reservation:*

Telephone: (418) 827-6873
Fax: (418) 827-6870

Achevé d'imprimer
en juin 2000
sur les presses de
Imprimerie H.L.N.

Imprimé au Canada – Printed in Canada